An Introduction
to
Protestant Theology

School of Divinity

Gardner-Webb University
School of Divinity

BOOKS BY HELMUT GOLLWITZER
Published by The Westminster Press

An Introduction to Protestant Theology
The Existence of God as Confessed by Faith

An Introduction
to
Protestant Theology

by
HELMUT GOLLWITZER

Translated by
DAVID CAIRNS

THE WESTMINSTER PRESS
Philadelphia

Translated from the German
*Befreiung zur Solidarität: Einführung in die
Evangelische Theologie*
© 1978 Chr. Kaiser Verlag München

This translation Copyright © 1982 David Cairns

BOOK DESIGN BY DOROTHY ALDEN SMITH

Published by
The Westminster Press®
Philadelphia, Pennsylvania

PRINTED IN THE UNITED STATES OF AMERICA
9 8 7 6 5 4 3 2 1

Library of Congress Cataloging in Publication Data

Gollwitzer, Helmut.
    An introduction to Protestant theology.

    Translation of: Befreiung zur Solidarität.
    Bibliography: p.
    1. Theology, Doctrinal—Introductions. 2. Theology,
Protestant. I. Title.
    BT65.G6413   1982   230'.044   82-4798
    ISBN 0-664-24415-7   AACR2

Contents

Preface

I cannot deny the resemblance. Karl Barth concluded his active teaching in Basel in the winter term of 1961–62 with a series of lectures entitled "Introduction to Evangelical Theology," and I did the same in my last term of regular teaching, the summer of 1975. As with Barth, this course was intended, not to add to the many existing introductions to the study of theology, but to provide a summary and record of my own theological journey—in short, a balancing of accounts which makes no claim to finality for myself or general validity for others. Indeed, concluding such a period of one's life recommends an attitude of modesty and an awareness of the provisional nature and the incompleteness of all our work and knowledge. The hope that my previous work might be useful to others includes the hope that such a rendering of accounts might be useful too.

Of course the content of this series of lectures is very different from that of Barth's lectures, just as two men are different, even though they have been in close association as teacher and pupil. It is a pleasure to the pupil, out of gratitude and love, to be able to point to agreement with the heritage of his teacher, even in his own further journey, but this must not hinder him from going his own way, even when differences appear. Whether these are differences only in emphasis and projection of lines of thought caused by the differences in time and in situation, or whether they amount to differences of substance, must become evident in each case, and on this point there will often be differences between the pupil and his critics.

While Karl Barth and Martin Luther have been my most important theological teachers, which is shown by the frequency of my quotations from them, this does not imply any lack of gratitude to many others to whom I also am indebted, even if I have failed to name them.

According to Max Liebermann, the secret of art is omission. I was forced to keep this in mind both by the shortness of the term and the need for clarity in this course of lectures. Hence the brevity of my lists of bibliographical references, which do not fully indicate which voices from the theological dialogue of the past and the present were in my mind from time to time. This selectivity also influenced my choice of themes, which was only partly dictated by the canon of the most important works on theological doctrine and was in part subjectively based on the direction of my own interests. This direction of interest imposed itself upon me largely through my position in a department that specializes in philosophy and the social sciences but also through my participation in the social movements and conflicts of our time, and through the composition of my audience which, together with a number who had fully or partly matriculated in theological courses, always contained a proportion of students from various other fields of study. This last circumstance was not only most stimulating for me but obliged me continually to translate specialized theological language into terms that could be generally understood. I hope this will make these lectures accessible and useful to readers who do not have previous acquaintance with theological terminology, and enable them to engage themselves with the problems discussed here if only their interest is keen enough.

Since these omissions were forced upon me, I can only ask my readers to confine themselves in their questioning to what is discussed here and the manner of its discussion, and not to criticize if they do not find a treatment here of the subject for which they were looking. I could not aim at an all-embracing delineation of even a single problem, let alone the whole field of theology. And it will also be understood that my purpose was to develop my own position, knowing well how controversial this is on many of the themes touched upon here.

The chapters of this book were originally delivered in a course of lectures, as stated, and were later worked over and expanded. The second chapter appeared in *Evangelical Commentaries*, September 1977; the sixth chapter was included as a contribution to the *Festschrift für Martin Fischer, Theologie und Kirchenleitung*, Munich, 1976, pp. 119–134.

A bibliography is appended to each chapter. It includes books by other writers, mostly contemporary, which have stimulated the development of my thinking in recent years. There are indeed only a few titles listed to assist the reader who would like to read more about the subject.

This book is dedicated to my friend Fritz Bissinger, who for many years was director of the publishing firm of Christian Kaiser. His retirement from active professional life (1977) almost coincided in time with the publication of this my last series of university lectures. We met for the first time in the Kaiser publishing firm's offices, when he entered it as an apprentice, and at a time when the firm had to be directed by my friend Otto Bruder-Salomon from a hidden back room because of his non-Aryan origin. Then we saw each other again in Berlin in the last years before the war, where he worked with the firm of Paul Neff and I stood in for the imprisoned Martin Niemöller in his Dahlem parish. When I returned home in the spring of 1950 from being a prisoner of war in Russia, we met again on the very next day in a circle of Bavarian friends, and since then we have gone on our way in close friendship, united by a large measure of agreement on church and political problems. It was principally through Bissinger that the firm of Kaiser has remained my publisher, and I have been constantly invited by him for friendly consultation. This dedication is designed to thank him and to wish him health and continued activity during the present phase of his life.

I owe the preparation of the text of these lectures for publication to the friendly help of P.i.R. Hannelotte Reiffen and Hertha von Klewitz-Niemöller, without whom my present literary activity would not be possible.

HELMUT GOLLWITZER

Berlin, April 1978

I

The Freedom and Commitment of Theology

Over and above its evangelical function, theology is also a university discipline. But can theology be a free critical science, obligated to truth alone, and at the same time a discipline in service of the faith and of the proclamation of the church? We approach this question first by probing the relationship of theology to philosophy and to the other special disciplines, and second by examining the relationship of theology to the church and its task. We arrive thereby at the conclusion that theology is an exemplary science of inquiry and can rightly serve the church only as such. Thus the dialectic of freedom and commitment in theological thinking reveals itself.

Theology and Philosophy

When one ceases to be the holder of a teaching chair of evangelical (systematic) theology, the question arises, what has one really been doing in such a post? The title "teaching chair" has been dropped as a result of some university changes which I greatly welcome; but since it described me for twenty-five years, I must render an account, which I also owe to those who were exposed to me as the holder of such a chair or shared in my activity as fellow workers and friends.

My task as holder of the chair was to teach theology—more precisely, evangelical theology, and still more precisely, systematic theology. Of these three, "evangelical" is the all-important word, as will, I hope, become apparent from all that follows. For what is here to be taught has a connection with an *euangelion*—a joyful message. "Teaching" is a word that has many different nuances of meaning. It can mean the teaching of the wise man, who imparts long-ripened experience and knowledge to his disciples: the teaching utterances of the Buddha and of the great Hasidim, for example. But the master craftsman also imparts teaching to his apprentices, and the professor of chemistry imparts teaching in his laboratory to his students. The teaching of wisdom on the one hand and the teaching of the skills of the craftsman and the scientific investigator on the other are very different methods of teaching, and the methods of learning are correspondingly different. How difficult it is to determine what theology really is can be seen from the fact that at different times it has been classed as akin to wisdom (*sapientia*) or akin to a scientific discipline (*scientia*). If this chair is one of evangelical theology, then the difficulty becomes particularly clear: how much of the gospel can be taught and learned in the sense that wisdom is taught, and how much in the sense that science is taught?

As if this difficulty were quite easy to solve, the teaching and the learning of theology have been institutionalized by means of academic teaching chairs, and fitted into a very rigid institutional structure in our universities, as if this were the same thing as the institutionalization of other intellectual activities—for example, the investigation of the botanic and the atomic spheres, or that of local history or of journalism.

There is another chair for which this inclusion is equally problematic, the chair of systematic philosophy. Thus:

1. What philosophy and theology really are is still an open question. (This is not the case with regard to the individual sciences just mentioned.) Indeed, the answer-

ing of this question is one of the principal tasks of philosophy and theology, and their different schools are distinguished precisely by the ways in which they answer it.

2. Related to this is the fact that the subjective element in philosophy and theology is incomparably greater than in the individual sciences, so that their character as sciences is even more a matter of contention than the concept of science itself. To put it more exactly, the concept of science becomes more questionable the farther it extends beyond the realm of the individual sciences and inquires what knowing (and also teaching and learning) really is. Teaching is an intersubjective activity, and human knowing is not less so. It unites people; and for that reason we endeavor to reach criteria of true knowledge which all of us can satisfy. For the idea has proved astonishingly suggestive—especially in modern times—that the intersubjectivity of thinking and knowing is more certainly assured, the more "objectively" it is achieved, the more it can be detached from the person of the thinker and investigator, the more it can be verified by everyone in possession of a sound mind. This is not the place to investigate this idea; that is being done in the contemporary debate over the theory of science. But it can be said that objective knowledge, such as is sought for in modern science, creates a maximum of quantitative and a minimum of qualitative intersubjective consensus, and this gives it a high value in making modest claims to obtain consensus, which we must not fail to satisfy. It is indeed quite an achievement when we are at least in agreement about the facts—even though concerning their interpretation, ordering, and consistency there will inevitably be disagreement. But only where a common conviction develops out of this dispute is an intersubjective agreement of higher quality reached, which is useful for the formation of a social group that lives with these

convictions and bears witness to them in society.

Thus it is relevant to the essential question of church unity if we are compelled to state that the subjective element is much greater in theology as in philosophy than in the individual sciences. The latter can make possible only a minimum of qualitative intersubjective unity, much less than is necessary for the unity of the church. To give theology an objectivity which is equal to that of the individual sciences (let us say a positivistic objectivity), in order to ensure the unity of the church— that is the aim of fundamentalism, which holds that theology has only to reproduce what is written in the Bible—and that, indeed, in the form of its last redaction, the *textus receptus*. But the aim of every traditionalist theology is similar when it confines itself to the interpretation, in a traditional manner, of certain fundamental texts which are acknowledged in a church as authoritative.

But Fichte's saying, "The philosophy one chooses depends on what kind of person one is,"[1] applies, in our experience of the history of theology, with equal relevance to theology. Does this mean that theology is hopelessly condemned to subjectivism, and that it can contribute nothing to the unity of the church and all the more therefore to its dissolution? Are the statements of the theologians, like those of the philosophers, nothing more than the most subjective personal confessions,[2] belonging more to the realm of *belles lettres* (and, indeed, to its most subjective lyrical form) than to the realm of rigorous objective disciplined science, and therefore to be valued poetically rather than scientifically? Such affinities must give us pause when we postulate the scientific nature of theology. But in spite of this, there must be an element here that transcends the individual. To search for it, and to establish its validity, is part of the philosophical task, and no less of the theologi-

cal task—especially if theology has to do with the unity of
the church, a question we shall still have to ask. Philosophy and theology are, even if in a very different way,
projects undertaken in fellowship, inasmuch as—in Hegel's language—they belong to "objective spirit." At the
same time, they are individual enterprises for which
each individual thinker is to be held responsible. The
fact that they can be pursued in fellowship speaks for a
more than subjective character in philosophy and theology, and the fact that this transsubjective element must be
continually sought anew shows how indelible the subjectivity involved here is.

When we see that the problems of philosophy and
theology are so similar, the distinction between them
becomes much less obvious than it is commonly thought
to be. What have I really been concerning myself with
since I matriculated in the summer of 1928 in Munich in
the faculty of philosophy, and in the following winter in
Erlangen in philosophy and theology, and since in the
summer of 1932—after Karl Barth diffidently asked me if
I was afraid of burning my philosophical bridges behind
me—I gave up my philosophical matriculation (though
not, of course, my concern with philosophy)? If one
thinks of the academic division of spheres of work, that
can be easily stated, and likewise if one thinks of the
customary differences of world outlook. But every attempt made hitherto has failed to draw an unambiguous
line between the disciplines, either by considering the
differences in method, or in presuppositions, or in criteria of truth.[3] Such definitions fail to cover the work of
great Christian thinkers like Augustine and Thomas
Aquinas, who thought and wrote before our academic
division of labor existed. But the same is true of modern
thinkers like Pascal, or the great representatives of German idealism, or Kierkegaard.

One could say that Christian theology understands

itself to be the true philosophy—that is, accepting the presupposition of revelation, it does not exclude itself from philosophy as such, but from a philosophy that limits itself to an atheism of method or goes astray through dogmatic atheism.[4] But this would mean, on the one hand, that philosophy was condemned to obligatory atheism and forbidden to raise the question about God; and, on the other hand, that theology was condemned to a quite different manner of thinking, whether one should call it "bound by authority," existential, or pneumatic. This is unsatisfactory on both sides.

Or could one say that philosophy is a special form of theology? That is the tendency of Wilhelm Weischedel's endeavor to construct a contemporary philosophical theology. "Theology" here would mean reflection on ultimate questions, and philosophy, so understood, could be conceived of either as the secularized form of earlier religious theology or as the provisional form of theology limited to what is naturally possible (Thomas Aquinas) or as thinking where the theological element is finally stated in conceptual form (Hegel). Representatives of both sides, however, have felt that this did not do them justice, and so even such propositions have not solved the problem.

It seems to me that more promising than involvement in this debate is the attempt to consider the more precise question: With what does Christian theology concern itself? The answer at first seems simple: With the Christian religion. But that it is far from simple is shown at once by these three questions:

1. Is anyone who concerns himself with the Christian religion therefore a theologian? And does Christian theology concern itself only with Christian religion?

2. What is the specific manner in which Christian theology concerns itself with Christian religion, and also, perhaps, with all sorts of other subjects?

3. What is Christian religion, anyway? What is its essential nature? How is it to be described in order that theological concern with it should be possible?

The questions show that the word "theological" contains considerable problems. It is not even specifically Christian, but is pre-Christian. The word *theologia* appears first in Plato (*Republic* II, 379, a5), who speaks of *tupoi peri theologias,* by which he means "viewpoints concerning the representation of the divine," which for him are "the true goal and center of his thinking."[5] In Aristotle the word gains a double aspect which is still determinative today: Theology for him is, in the first place, the *prima philosophia,* the knowledge of the highest principles, the heart and goal of metaphysics (as it is today also in Wilhelm Weischedel's philosophical theology); in the second place, it is teaching about the gods as it is found, for example, in Hesiod—that is, mythical-poetic language about God, which then becomes a problem in metaphysics and receives intellectual clarification, so that "philosophy begins at the point where theology leaves off."[6] (Compare Hegel's transition from the picture thinking of theology to the conceptual thinking of philosophy.)

Thus we get a preliminary view of a problem that accompanies the whole history of Christian theology, the problem of the universality and particularity of Christian theology. Theology in the first sense mentioned by Aristotle is the question about "God"—not about the gods, nor even about the many conceptions of God or beliefs about him, which in many ways compete with one another, but the question about the ultimate, all-determining reality, about the final ground, the final goal and the highest being, which holds the world together in its inner core. As such it is identical with philosophy. These considerations have led today to the proposal of Wolfhart Pannenberg[7] to understand theology as an en-

deavor of thought embracing all religions and philoso-
phies, which has as its object the investigation of their
questions and answers. Its task is, first, to understand
these questions and answers, and then critically to inquire how far the answers given from time to time prove
themselves to be true within the perspective of our time
and at the level required by contemporary problems.

In contrast with such a challenge, a theology that
claims to be Christian and loyal to the Christian church
seems all too particular and limited. It loses the universal
perspective, however strenuously it may claim to possess
it with a pretension to finality that now appears to be
artificially inflated and dictated in an authoritarian manner. Thus it also loses its kinship with philosophy as an
intellectual enterprise which aims at finality and completeness, and it approaches rather the standing of the
individual positive sciences, inasmuch as now its object
is an individual one positively supplied to it—i.e., the
Christian religion, or, indeed, merely one of its confessional expressions.

But with this it might even run the risk of losing the
character of science. For now everything depends on the
answer given to our second question: In what manner
does Christian theology deal with its object, Christianity
thus delimited?

One way it can do this is in a historical manner, as
Adolf von Harnack[8] has proposed. Through inquiry into
the origin and the historical evolution of the Christian
religion together with its different embodiments, it
reaches a concept of the essence of Christianity and is
then able to use this concept critically in order to
pronounce judgment upon its different manifestations.
By adopting such a historical, phenomenological, and
morphological procedure, it would, however, have
dropped entirely the question about God, which linked it
with philosophy, and the question concerning final truth

and reality, which is its own motive and not merely that of the men and groups that it investigates.

Alternatively, it can hold fast to this question and find it answered in the Christian religion—i.e., in that Christian confession to which the particular theologian adheres—and thus can justify its self-limitation as Christian theology. Thus it declares that the answer which is to be found here is identical with final truth and rejects as impossible in principle any attempt to call it into question when it is asked from a standpoint external or superior to it. The identity of the particular with the universal is the thesis of such a theology of revelation. It has indeed managed to preserve its universality, but—as it appears to us—by the violent means of an authoritarian claim which can only call for blind obedience. But that separates it both from philosophy and from science in the modern sense. For here thought consists in search, not in possession. But this theology is, as it seems, in possession, and for that reason can only be defensive, and not critical. Under the influence of such a positivist[9] theology of religion Ludwig Feuerbach wrote:

> Science frees the spirit, enlarges heart and mind. But theology confines and limits them. . . . The theologian who takes up such a standpoint has no understanding of the scientific spirit or of theoretic freedom. He has gone to wrack and ruin as far as science is concerned, for he continually drags the theoretical into the realms of religion and morality; doubt to him is wickedness and sin; science has for him only a formal significance. However much he may profess his loyalty to it he does not take it seriously, because he takes seriously only his faith and the teachings of his church. Science to him is essentially shadow play, however strenuous an activity it may appear to be; his scholarship is a whited sepulcher. He has no genuine theoretic interest—faith has already taken

captive his theoretic interest. His only interest is practical; science is to him only a means to faith. His pursuit of science is impure, servile in its intention, and contrary to the spirit of science.[10]

If there were only these two possibilities, the outlook would be poor for a theology whose intention is frankly Christian. It would then be a fettered kind of thinking and thus a further proof of the thesis of modern rationalism which is so frequently represented, i.e., that faith and freedom, God and freedom, are incompatible. There have frequently been theologians who in this dilemma have stood defiantly on the side of constraint and denounced man's struggle for freedom and autonomy as religiously—and of course also politically—dangerous, unfitting for man, and thus rebellious and destructive.

It will later be necessary to show that it is not a secret capitulation to the modern spirit, but rather, the gospel itself which forbids us to opt thus for constraint and affirms our conviction today that such an option is simply intolerable. The modern longing for autonomy is caused by the conditions of the time, by the alliance of the church with dominant repressive social forces, and by the consequent denunciation of all efforts at emancipation as unchristian and antichristian. Often expressing itself in opposition to the church and to religion, it is, rather, a question posed to the church and to theology. We are asked whether, in view of the connection between the gospel and human freedom which the New Testament everywhere makes clear (John 8:31–36; Gal. 5:1–13), we cannot develop an understanding of these efforts which is helpful to them in their undeniable dangers and problems, instead of merely negating them.

Then indeed a Christian theology must be possible which does not fall victim to this dilemma—either free inquiry into matters of final concern, or servile thought which submits to established courts of appeal. But this dilemma takes for granted the alternative: Theology is in any case thought which, in the search for final realities, has committed itself in such a way that it *either* acknowledges "no authority but its own in the freedom of its inquiry"[11] *or else* submits to an authoritatively given answer which it has only to defend as satisfying its questions. Even the latter alternative is only a special case—granted, a particularly questionable one—of the presupposition that in both instances we have to deal with expressions of the metaphysical need which is innate in the human spirit, expressions which are, however, in competition as free and unfree thinking, and between which we are compelled to choose, whether we optimistically venture for freedom or resignedly believe that we limited human beings must accept restrictions.

Theology and the Church

In order to come to a more satisfying answer to the problem, let us ask what is the relationship of theology to that power which until now has appeared to be the cause of its bondage, the church. Biographically, the metaphysical need of which we spoke will have played a considerable part in determining the way in which a person one day comes to be a theologian, even a professional university theologian. But there is another factor of at least as great importance, i.e., that one day we come to be conscious members of the Christian church. Either we were born into it and, as is customary, were baptized into it as infants, grew up in it, and remained in it, without any deep rupture having separated us from it, or we came into it through personal development in a variety of ways. What has attracted us so that, in spite of all crises and criticisms of the church, we deliberately count ourselves as belonging to it? One can mention various things: a forcible impression made upon us by its message, our attraction to the life of the Christian fellowship, the experience of cultus and worship, encounter with impressive Christian personalities, and so on. At any rate, the result is that now we count ourselves as members of it, and that in consequence we participate in the activities, the problems and needs of this fellowship, and share in responsibility for it. Then soon we find that theology is one of the vital necessities of this fellowship. How so?

That in itself is nothing exceptional. Every known fellowship is a context of shared meanings. We must communicate in language about every interaction, and this in itself makes a minimum of theory necessary. A football club is constituted by an understanding of games in general, and of the game of football in particular. Laws have to be drawn up, techniques of play studied, and new ones developed. All this involves a mass of theoretical work, which is set down in authoritative regulations, which must then be reinterpreted and critically tested from time to time. In a political party this happens to a much greater extent, inasmuch as here the procedure involves more verbal interaction with trains of thought, ideologies, analyses, and proposals for action and propaganda.

Every human fellowship needs verbal communication, an agreement about ends and means, the formulation of agreed conclusions in authoritative texts, a discipline of interpretation to protect its identity through historical changes, a process of self-criticism to secure the convergence of practice with the declared ideal, a polemic against deformation of its nature, and a defense against challenges from without.

The case of the Christian church is exactly similar. Theology comes into existence primarily because this group as a human group requires a theory. Concentration on questions concerning Christianity must not at once be regarded as proof of an imperialistic claim to infallibility, but arises simply from the service which theology has to perform for this group. Whether theology is meaningful depends entirely on whether or not the existence of this group is regarded as meaningful and to be welcomed.

Then, further, it is clear that theology is only in the second place the task of certain members of the group; primarily it is the task of all. For all are interested in the life of their group and consequently in the necessary theoretical clarification, and everyone must decide for himself in contentious matters. How theology is developed depends on how this group—or a group within this group—understands itself, and this again depends on the self-understanding that is achieved by theology. Thus, between theology and church there is a hermeneutic circle, inasmuch as theology arises from the practice of the church and from its practical needs, and then, as the theory of the practice, reacts again upon the church.

The church, however, is a very special group. It did not come together like a club or a political party in order to realize a particular end, or to protect particular human interests; but it is a group called into being, called together, and constituted by a message—and indeed a universal message! This means that theology is necessary for the church in a far higher degree than theory, however rudimentary, is necessary for a football club. For the church's origin in such a message demands:

a. The understanding of this message and thus a common understanding of the fellowship concerning it.

b. A life of the fellowship in accordance with the message.

c. The promulgation of this message (which is not esoteric, but is meant for all) to other people, and consequently its translation into the different human languages and situations.

1. From this point we can see that it is impossible for the intellect to be excluded. The content that must be

expressed here is not merely the content of an irrational experience, which might find its most adequate expression in music, as the young Schleiermacher believed. It is the content of a message that was uttered in language and has to be passed on in language. The attempt has repeatedly been made in Christendom to malign and eliminate thought, understanding, and reason, in contrast with faith, but for good reason it has never been able to win the day. There is no Christian faith which can feel at home in an irrational darkness, in the night of the Romantics. There is, indeed a great deal of unreasonable Christianity which fears the clarity of reason, but no legitimately unreasonable Christianity. Christian faith loves the light, even the *lumen rationis;* for this reason it has an affinity with the movements of enlightenment in human history.[12] The question to which Christian faith gives rise is, at the most, whether *our* reason is really reasonable, whether our understanding is really so ready to understand, so free, open, and unprejudiced as its concept requires. Thus there is no Christian existence which excludes intellect and reflection, or even belittles it.

2. Similarly, there is no Christian experience which excludes communication. If we were considering only the metaphysical question, then this might also—and perhaps best—be pondered in the isolation of the hermit, or experienced and answered in the solitary and ineffable experiences of the mystic. Nothing is to be said against either, just as times of solitude can be specially fruitful for each of us. But Christian theology has its origin in the peremptory needs of a group called "the church," which has been brought together by a message into a special life of fellowship and furnished with a special commission to the outside world. The individuals are woven together into this group life by communication and exist in accordance with a message only through

communication. Christian theology can thus only be a social concern; it can never be a solitary concern, however much we may from time to time become lonely in our participation in this social concern, and isolated in the church.

3. That this can happen even to the theologian is connected with the fact that the use of the intellect in conjoint effort inevitably has a critical function also. The service of theology in the church does not only mean criticism, but it inevitably includes it. Rightly pursued, theology is the church's self-criticism. Hence the formula "Theology is a function of the church," which is used equally by Karl Barth and Paul Tillich, among others, is saved from conformist misunderstanding.

This formula could be understood as a positivism of revelation, in the manner sketched above. That is to say, the message describes a situation of the church as it ought to be. By means of this feedback of theology, the church as it is is compared with the church as it ought to be, and is corrected in accordance with the latter. This sounds at first quite simple in cybernetic jargon. The history of the church, however, shows the difficulties concealed in it. It is easy to seek for what ought to be in some place where it is tangibly present, and at any moment capable of recall—perhaps in the revealed fundamental store of affirmations, formulated in propositions, which regulate how the church should live (order, hierarchy, cultus) and what it should pass on as doctrine. The task of theology is, then, to support the authorities established by revelation by proving that they themselves and their decisions are founded on the affirmations of revelation and are in conformity with them, while at the same time nailing down and correcting incorrect elements, which may creep in, by comparing them with the canon of the authoritative texts of revelation.

This conception of theology corresponds to a similar conception of revelation in which revelation is regarded as the disclosure (ordained by God and bestowed on the church) of a series of truths otherwise inaccessible to human understanding (*veritates revelatae*). These truths are contained in the Bible, and in the oral traditions of faith, though admittedly in a rather enigmatic manner, so that an authority empowered to interpret, a "living teaching office," is thought to be needed in order to make accessible the store of truths present in this twofold tradition. In this view theology is an auxiliary science which collaborates with this teaching office and interprets its decisions and defends them.

One thing is clear: Revelation and the teaching office are here thought of as belonging to the same structure of authority. They speak in propositions, and when they have spoken, nothing remains but to submit: *Roma locuta, causa finita* ("Rome has spoken, the matter is decided"). The old Protestant theology put the verbally inspired Bible in the place of the papacy in an attempt to free men from such human domination (just as contemporary fundamentalism does). And for the same reason the confessional Lutheranism of the nineteenth century regarded the Augsburg Confession as the norm of biblical exposition. But in both cases, in spite of such change, the authoritarian structure remained unchanged.

But the God-man event of which the Bible speaks can be understood in a very different manner. (It is the event described by the word "revelation," which is not central in the biblical vocabulary.) Such a change in the interpretation of revelation also means a change in the way in which theology is understood. For the Reformers, especially for Martin Luther, it is not *truths* that are disclosed, but *one* truth, the encounter of God and man which creates fellowship between God and man, and at the same time between man and man, giving each access to the other. It comes through a word spoken, as Luther emphasizes, which convicts man in his conscience—a word that is indeed spoken by men (through its transmission by the church) but is so absolute that man knows through it what he really is: he sees himself brought to a halt by God, exposed by God, and wholly thrown upon God's mercy. For the fellowship thus opened up Karl Barth uses the fundamental biblical term "covenant," a fellowship already revealed in creation, and, after the breach caused by sin, which is here laid bare, revealed anew by the forgiveness that issues through the cross of Jesus Christ. This word "covenant" goes beyond Luther's central concept of justification and shows that what is at stake is God's fellowship with every individual and at the same time with the whole of humanity.[13]

The church can and must play its part as a servant in the creation of this fellowship. It has its own origin in the event of such fellowship and it plays its part by repeating the biblical witness to this situation of encounter between God and man, and by continually reactivating it in every new situation in time.

Acting "as a servant" means that neither the church nor theology has this event under its control. They cannot themselves bring it about, nor can they dispose of it as inherited capital, nor invest it and make some profit by it, nor can they claim for themselves a monopoly over it, as if this event could be achieved only by their mediation; they can only indicate it by serving as witnesses, and by placing this indication as an instrument (*medium ac instrumentum*) at the disposal of him who alone can bring this event to pass. That is what is meant in the doctrine of the Trinity, when the Holy Spirit is spoken of as the one who himself and alone makes what is promised in the word of revelation an operative reality among us.

Thus church and theology (as Karl Barth used to say)

stand between memory and expectation. By means of the memory held fast by earlier witnesses, of that which this reality has already brought to pass, they mobilize in expectation of future fulfillment, drawing other men into this expectation by this act of witness. In order to help the service of the church, theology has to reflect on what is meant by the event which is remembered and promised by the basic witness of the Bible, how its operation is connected with the event which is called Jesus Christ, and what consequences that has for our views on man, on history, on life between birth and death, on nature, on the problems of society, and on the tasks and dangers of our lives.

But if theology does not have this complex event in its grasp, and if the event of revelation, as it operates in concrete time from moment to moment upon concrete men, is connected with the one event of the historical person Jesus Christ—an event which theology, in spite of all the research possible and necessary, does not have in its grasp either—then that is a very remarkable situation for the kind of human thinking which theology must undertake.

This situation has one presupposition. That is the promise of the covenant which is given in the memory handed down in tradition, and which evokes expectation; its name is Jesus Christ. In contrast with the presupposition of an individual science, which consists in the tangible nature of its object in its knowability for men (and this is a matter for reflection by philosophical epistemology), in this event only the memory and report of those who have experienced it are tangible. But this report refers beyond itself to the intangible reality to which it bears witness—and that is why we speak of "witness." And the witness must ever be questioned anew concerning this reality that transcends it. Ever anew, for the reference must be repeated afresh in every time and for every time. All human words and sentences must ever anew be pressed into the service of this ever-new reference.

Thus theology is not less an inquiring science than others. When it is conducted rightly, it fulfills the challenge presented to every science, ever anew to call into question itself, its methods, and its hitherto accepted results and formulae, and to do so in an exemplary manner. The question is continually reopened as to what its accepted language about God and man, about that event of encounter we spoke of, and about Jesus Christ, really means, what is the reality indicated by the words and sentences used hitherto: God, revelation, Jesus Christ, word of God, sin, forgiveness, justification, covenant, redemption, the Kingdom of God, faith, love, the church, etc. How to speak rightly about it, with some prospect of agreement with that reality to which we bear witness, what are the conditions and methods of inquiry—all this must perpetually be made the subject of new inquiry. Granted, this cannot happen without reference to history—here no more than in any other discipline. It is not as if inquiry had only begun today, and as if contemporary inquiry and old "dogmas" were set against each other in opposition. And it is not as if men from the beginning, who were touched by revelation, had not been made to embark on an intensive inquiry, in a discussion, admittedly a critical discussion, with those who looked back in memory to the event, and proclaimed it in hopeful expectation. All these men were searching for the human echo that answers that event, and were thus involved in discussion with the church of earlier days, with the "fathers" and their Christian contemporaries.

Theology is *bound* to the fundamental witness without which this specific inquiry would not exist, the Bible.

We shall have to deal with this later, and with the fact that, because of the peculiar nature of the fundamental witness and our obligation which results from it, our inquiry cannot be transformed into the knowledge of a store of quotable statements, and can proceed only within the limits of well-defined dogmatic precedents which are to be determined beforehand. For we must first discover the intention of the message contained in the texts, and we must seek ever anew for its interpretative key.[14]

As an example of such an understanding of theology we may name Karl Barth's *Church Dogmatics*. This may perhaps be surprising to many. That theology is a function of the church (Barth does not usually fail to insert the word "critical") does not at all mean that, taking a positivistic attitude to revelation, its task is to supervise a fundamental store of church dogmas and set them before us with the harsh injunction "Accept or be damned!" as Dietrich Bonhoeffer mistakenly assumed. This work, with its ever-renewed formulations, even with its explicit and implicit self-corrections, is a single sustained invitation to proper inquiry, an example of sound, unbiased theological method. At the same time, it provides an example of such inquiry, and by so doing constitutes a transformation of what dogmatics and dogmatic teaching is commonly understood to be, and thus stands in contradiction to every kind of dogmatism. This holds good even for those parts which are written in the language of affirmation and assertion, and in which reflection passes over into the language of preaching. These bring into view what is set before our inquiry as its object, and suggest how the appropriate human echo to it might be formulated. Understood in this way, Barth's *Dogmatics* is a perfect example of theology understood as a "hypothetical" science, such as Wolfhart Pannenberg claims it should be.[15]

The *obedience* of theology does not consist in repeating what is dictated, by recitation or by heteronomous thinking, but in thoroughly independent inquiry—even though this is directed toward something that has been declared to us—about the witness that was borne in remembrance and promise. It does not consist in the development of our own axioms and premises, or those handed to us by philosophy, as indeed has repeatedly happened in theological history. It is in this sense that Calvin's word is to be understood: "All true knowledge of God is born out of obedience."[16]

Theology, like every other science, is obedient to the fulfillment of its task, from which it does not allow itself to be deflected by any other authority—whether ecclesiastical or extra-ecclesiastical. It receives its task through the mediation of the church, which has need of it. But that task is not to justify the empirical being of the church, neither its persons nor their actions nor their ordinances nor their doctrines. Its task is, rather, to test these critically by the message to which the church owes its existence. The special dialectic of constraint and freedom, which is peculiar to theology, and which can admittedly make it a very irritating and stimulating partner in the house of the human sciences, arises from the fact that the message cannot be applied as a criterion in a straightforward manner, because—like its object, the revelation—it must be sought for ever anew. If that does not happen, then we are operating with all sorts of miraculous words and propositions imposed on us by tradition, whose meaning remains obscure to us, and which for that very reason require blind submission. Such a procedure is anything but evangelical, and has nothing to do with bearing witness to the gospel. It is in fact not only joyless but boring in addition. But what is the origin of the inquiry, and in what direction must it go? This question will make us realize the unique significance of the Bible for church and theology; a future chapter will deal with it.

It should, however, be clear by now that the freedom of theology—which it, like all scientific thinking, requires—has its foundation precisely in the fact that we must ever anew ask for the message, for its authentic content and meaning, and consequently can come into conflict about it among ourselves, and in the fact that we have nothing under our control from the beginning. For there is no church authority which for any reason could have it more under control, and which for that reason could prescribe to theology its results. Other persons, even other members of the church, can only ask those in the church who are in a special way commissioned for theological work whether and how far they dedicate themselves to this singular task, and then, since *everyone* in the church is concerned with theology, test for themselves whether helpful clarifications arise from their efforts.

Thus theological concentration on the question of the Christian message which is the foundation of the church itself, and on the obligation to serve the church, is not based, as it earlier appeared, on the presupposition of an *absolute claim* made by Christianity—as if Christians already possessed the knowledge that the revelation of God in Jesus Christ is the sole and universal truth. Not even a theologian knows that from the beginning, or once and for all. The theologian does indeed hear the witness of the Bible—and the believing witnesses of the church—refer to Jesus Christ as the sole and perfect salvation of all people. But the theologian must begin ever anew to ask what these words of other men mean, how they come to make such extraordinary claims and how they establish them, and what is the relationship to them of other faith claims, religious and philosophical. The fact that we can obtain from contemporary theologians no unambiguous answer on this point, but that the conflict mentioned above continues, is indeed a sign that here science is not (as Ludwig Feuerbach's polemic asserted) operating under dictated premises. It is a sign, rather, that the material for study—the assertion of the biblical witnesses transmitted by the church—has become a task for thought which does not imprison thinking or cut it short, but sets it in motion.

Of course, wherever the task of thinking is laid upon us, there is the threat of intellectualization and of the isolation of theory from practice. This will show itself (*a*) in an audacity of thought which claims to grasp living reality in concepts to such an extent that inquiry—which is directed to the still unconceptualized reality that resists absorption into a conceptual system—achieves its end, so that it can only go on repeating itself endlessly. We have then rational formulae, in which the mystery of reality—nay (the climax of audacity!), the mystery of *this* reality—is deciphered, known, and confessed. And so reality—yes, and of all things *this* reality—no longer resists us, and we are protected from surprises. (This is the suspicious thing about the program of Hegel's philosophy of religion.)

From this follows (*b*) the encroachment of theology on life: the church of the theologians, in which the theologians dictate to the others what they have to believe, and in which faith degenerates into the repetition of true propositions.

Thus the importance of theology for the church corresponds to its modesty. The modesty of theology means that it may not bind anyone to itself. Its task as the servant of all who pay attention to it is to help them to hear the gospel themselves, and to inquire themselves, but to hear and inquire in this concentrated way, directing their attention to the message. So there is some truth in the statement with which the liberal Basel church historian Eberhard Vischer concluded a lecture fifty years ago on "The Task of Theological Science" (1927): "The task of theological science is ever and again to save us from theology."

RECOMMENDED READING

Buri, Fritz; Lochman, Jan Milic; and Ott, Heinrich. *Dogmatik im Dialog.* Vol. 2 of *Theologie—Offenbar-ung—Gotteserkenntnis.* 1974.

Gollwitzer, Helmut, and Weischedel, Wilhelm. *Denken und Glauben.* 1964.

Janowski, Hans Norbert, and Stammler, Eberhard (eds.). *Was ist los mit der deutschen Theologie?* 1978.

Pannenberg, Wolfhart. *Wissenschaftstheorie und Theologie.* 1973.

Picht, Georg. *Der Gott der Philosophen und die Wissenschaft der Neuzeit.* 1966.

Picht, Georg, and Rudolph, Enno (eds.). *Theologie—was ist das?* 1977.

Sauter, Gerhard (ed.). *Theologie als Wissenschaft.* Theologische Bücherei, No. 43. 1970.

II   Theory and Practice as a Problem of Contemporary Theology

The establishment of theology as a university science is a phenomenon of the ever-increasing specialization in the work of society. But in this society, specialization is bound up with social privilege. If the theologians belong to a privileged class in society, that can have a deleterious effect on their work. For this reason other forms of theology, epecially those which originate in the deprived countries of our contemporary world, are important for us. They stimulate us to create a theology in our society which may counteract the domination of experts and social privilege.

Theology is neither the mother nor the ruler but the servant of Christian faith and life, precisely in its nature as critical thought and inquiry. The church's life is drawn not from theology but from proclamation of the message uttered by those who have been apprehended by it. Theology is a supplementary concern. As theory, it stands between practice and practice.

Historically the church began as the practice of a new life, called into being by the message; and this still happens today. For the church's life, both internally and externally (as transmitter of the message), is lived in communication, since faith concerns the whole person and is concerned to make one mature and intelligent (*fides quaerens intellectum,* "faith that seeks to understand"). Since the practice of faith, both in individual life and in social life, encounters many problems which we must solve responsibly for ourselves, the church stands in continual need of new theoretical formulations. For this reason it is disastrous if the church and its members are equipped only with earlier theory, for that cannot produce a practical echo to the message today, only an inadequate or even a reactionary one.

Thus situated as church theology is between practice and practice, its traditional organization as an academic discipline appears questionable. It is, however, taken so much for granted that people hardly reflect about its problematic nature or about its conditions and its results. The challenge to become practical, and the relevance of theory in theology to practice, was dinned into the ears of university teachers in the years of student unrest, and today many are glad that their implacable resistance to it proved successful. It contained, of course, many fallacies—contempt of theory, pragmatism, and also lack of interest in matters of faith—which made its rejection easy, without the deeper questions involved being taken seriously.

This question, however, is implied even by the canonical texts, the most important subject matter for the work of theology as an interpretative discipline. In great part— e.g., in the whole of the New Testament—these texts grew out of situations altogether different from those which produce our academic writings. Their authors do not live a separate existence, isolated from their groups. What they write originates in the life of the group itself; the questions they answer are vital questions arising from the practice of the group. The hardships, temptations, and joys of the group are immediately shared by these authors, and they share them immediately as wandering preachers, as spokesmen, as those first exposed to the assaults of the surrounding world. The researchers of the form-historical school, working within the sociological category of "community theology," were the first to draw attention to the way in which whole communities participated in the creation of theology. There was indeed specialization of function among them, but theology still took form in them in a manner not entailing such specialization.

With the infiltration of Hellenistic intellectuals into the early church, this situation changed. The attentive reader of the first volume of Harnack's *History of Dogma* can observe how much the needs of these men determined the formation of theology. At the same time, the church began to organize itself hierarchically, and, in order to exclude heterodox groups, to develop theology as an instrument for the demarcation and legitimization of hierarchical power—precisely by means of the schools of these intellectuals. This prepared the way for a form of theology that was necessary for the church, which since Constantine has been in alliance with the dominant powers of society; it paralleled the specialization of tasks in society, in which a staff of intellectuals was entrusted with the business of theory. An order of specialists dominates over the unlettered, an *ecclesia activa* over the *ecclesia passiva*, the clergy over the laity, who have been relieved of theological responsibility and held in subjection. Thus theology appears as the construction of a theory which makes itself independent of the life of the lay world. Theology can be engaged in before practice and without reference to it; it is a discipline with its own circle of independent problems, whose elaboration satisfies the ingenuity of theological specialists, but it is often far removed from the problems that are of burning concern to the real practice of the church and its people.

In the churches of the Reformation, in spite of Luther's proclamation of the Christian fellowship as the supreme authority in the judgment of doctrine, nothing essential was changed. On this point Adolf Schlatter, in his study *Der Dienst des Christen in der älteren Dogmatik* (The service of the Christian in the early dogmatics), with which in 1897 he began his series of *Beiträge zur Förderung christlicher Theologie* (Contributions to the advancement of Christian theology), remarked with great acumen: "It followed from the standpoint of the early writers that they had no essential interest in the Christian community. The clerical office is indispensable, because the Word must be proclaimed, but not so the fellowship, because even without it one can believe and love. . . . Participation in the church in their opinion did not entail for the believer any call to service. For in relation to the church the believer is related only as a recipient, not as a giver. . . . To the man who is neither a member of the clergy nor an authority, God has allotted no service in the church." If then in modern times "the believer's appreciation of the church" as the "servant of divine grace" has grown dim, the reason is "not wholly, but partly because it never completely understood, and so did not perform, the service committed to it when it was left entirely in the hands of the clergy."[17]

Schlatter's words point up the fact that the academic degeneration of theology is closely connected with the status of the clerical office and with the restriction of preaching to the ministerial sermon. The theological faculties have been institutions for the education of owners of the preaching monopoly—a monopoly whose function was to bring these owners under the control of church and state authority and to prevent the independent theological thought of "lay" persons from making the Christian congregations cells of unrest in the social order. At the same time, the faculties took part in the growth of the university discipline, which in its turn results from the further development of the specialization of labor in society. Thus the isolation of theology from the life of the church and from everyday life is due both to the status of the clerical office and to its own participation in the university disciplines. And there is a corresponding inferiority complex of the lay person in theological matters as well as an inferiority complex of the theologian in nontheological matters. Both fear they will appear to be dilettantes and amateurs. The consequence of this is the declaration by both sides that the church (i.e., the theological and ecclesiastical authorities) is incompetent to deal with matters outside the realm of theology, and the surrender of these areas as being under the jurisdiction of their own special laws.

This should not lead to the conclusion that the division of labor in society should be abolished without more ado, as if we could quite simply return to the period that preceded the specialization of work and knowledge in modern times. But the decisive question is whether the conditions and the effects of specialization have been at all realized and reflected upon self-critically, and whether, in consequence, a movement follows which seeks to neutralize these effects and to escape from the restrictions caused by them. If the church is to conceive of itself as a Christian fellowship—i.e., as a group in which the relationships of subordination between Jew and Greek, master and servant, male and female are canceled out (Gal. 3:28), and in which accordingly there can be no domination of the ignorant by the experts—then this implies the duty of forming a counter group in an ever more strongly specialized society that is degenerating from a democracy into a society governed by experts. In this counter group all members share in and help to determine the common life, developing their capacities by this participation. Thus we shall break with the myth that has been dinned into us ever since our school days "that in all activities there are specialists, with whom we can never compete, and that if we are to achieve anything, we must make ourselves experts."[18]

On account of the Catholic monopoly of the priesthood

and the Protestant monopoly of the preacher, the theologians were especially exposed to the effects of the division of labor. This is, however, simultaneously an allocation or a refusal of privilege (at least in every society of privileges). And these privileges are also very material. Elitist in contrast with the nonacademic classes, and materially secure, theologians and theology have an extraterritorial status in the struggle for existence that rages around them, and they become at the same time a part of the privileged class, with whose ways of thinking and interests they are much more closely identified than they for the most part can realize and acknowledge. We theologians are deeply stamped by this membership of a privileged class, and by our elitist status of independence over against the broad lower classes, in our language in the first place and then in our way of working. It is absolutely imperative that we discard this class-determined manner of thinking, feeling, and working, and this elitist isolation, if the claim that theology as a function of the church is to have any practical content, and if Gal. 3:28 is to be more than the mere description of an illusory church ideology. For this reason it is just as important for theology as it is for the lay person to discard this dualism of lay person and expert, and for this reason it is not removed simply by theologians holding training schools for the laity.

"Thanks to its privileged position, theology today is less exposed to experiences of alienation than most other activities, which, in economic respects, are subject to harder laws and compulsions. Therefore in this country theology at best sympathizes with and does not experience the compulsion of the experiences of alienation which are the fate of the majority of our contemporaries today, and which find varied and articulate expression in literature."[19]

In a similar vein Paulo Freire writes: "Only reflect

upon this contradiction: I speak of brotherliness, and yet I am an intellectual, equipped with rights of my own, which the worker does not have. 'Good,' someone might say, 'Paulo, you are still a brother, but on another plane.' But that is only an academic way of pushing this difference aside. And the same is true with reference to teaching and learning, for how can the teacher who stands on his dignity as a professor be a brother to his students? He is so far away from his students. He has 'knowledge,' and because he possesses knowledge he thinks that he must impart knowledge to the students. So these teachers are not brothers, but as 'possessors' they are instructors. In order to give up the role, in order to become a real brother, I must change the whole of society."[20]

In fact, this brings a comprehensive change of society into view, and perhaps the fear of such a change, which would abolish our privileges, is the reason why I cannot parallel these two quotations with any from the realm of academic theology. If there are any, at least they have not been brought to my attention, and that would be evidence of their scarcity. This also explains why, under the challenge of student unrest, the attitude of the teaching staff of the theological faculties was in no way different from that of other faculties. The question raised here, whether the teaching activity in theology should not be fundamentally different from that of the other sciences which supply the necessary experts to bourgeois society for its production and reproduction, was just as little recognized and discussed as was the teachers' own implication in, and usefulness to, this privileged society.

This explains, too, why increasingly those parts of the Christian community which are outside bourgeois society—that is, the churches of the third world—attest to the inapplicability of our theological work which in the past was successfully exported to them. They tell us that it is far too abstract and has no real bearing on their life problems. This is the message they have been sending us for years. One can reply to such criticisms with the same arguments we used to defend the necessity of thorough historical research and of reflection on a high level of abstraction against the pragmatism of students in the early terms of their study. But there remains always a residue which should be disquieting to us. For it must be supposed that these manifestations of dissatisfaction are not merely the expression of an increasing self-awareness, of an increasing reflection upon their own cultural conditions, and, in consequence, a sense of the *cultural* conditioning of our reputedly universally valid manner of theological thinking, but that they are also expressions of a sense of the *social* conditioning of our theological thinking by our privileged situation. This situation makes possible a biblical exegesis which pays attention only to the historical derivation of ideas and which ignores the way in which the texts reflect social conflicts and, consequently, shows not the slightest awareness of their relevance to situations today which, for example, spring to the eyes of the fishermen of Solentiname. On this point one should consult Ernesto Cardenal's book.[21]

This situation makes possible the abstraction of questions of faith and of the problems posed for Christian faith by pressing material problems, which makes the original connection between the two planes almost unrecognizable. Thus, not only in the lands of greatest material need but among us also, ministers educated in this manner are hard put, in their daily concern with problems of rent, unemployment, schoolboy suicide, alcoholism, etc., to restore this connection. Thus it becomes possible to reflect on the message that God is love without giving even a passing thought to our complicity in the grim compulsion to which our economic system subjects other peoples for our advantage. That the ordinary person—who undoubtedly is as much the concern of many a theological author as is his own specialist colleague—is at the same time, as a shareholder in the Volkswagen company, guilty of sharing in the profits earned by the murderous exploitation of the campesinos and indios in the Amazon territory—of all this the theological author usually knows almost nothing, and for this reason his reflection on the significance of the love of God for our life has limitations. But those Christians in the third world, who earlier had been grateful recipients of our theology, are now aware of these limits and today refuse to accept it.

They perceive in their church environment that our theology does not counteract their own dangers—the dangers, namely, of apathy in the face of the distress that surrounds them, of flight into religious byways, and of the temptation to accommodate themselves to the powers that be—but rather increases them. And they experience in their special situations the rise and development of another kind of theology, very much less individualistic, not in the least elitist, and clearly analogous to the primitive Christian situation of which we have spoken. There, where Christian practice is immediately confronted with human distress, struggle, and hope, in the slums and in the context of anticolonial and social movements of liberation, there emerge (we experienced repeatedly a similar situation in our resistance to Nazism) theoretical questions of the most varied kinds for committed Christian groups, for whose further practice an answer is immediately urgent. In finding this answer the whole group plays its part; professional theologians as members of such groups have no longer a dominating but only an advisory function, and their theological thinking is done in the closest proximity to the questions arising out of the practice of their group. In this way the Latin-American theology of liberation and the American and African black theology came into being.

It is not a case of romantically and artificially transferring ourselves into such conditions, which would be impossible. But from this, if ecumenism means that everything concerns everybody, certain conclusions can and must be drawn. The first would be to learn from this to be modest and recognize our own relativity. The kind of theology that dominates in our situation is neither the only way nor the best way of doing theology. We academic theologians should therefore be interested in discovering and fostering other forms of current theological inquiry and reflection in the evangelical academies, in circles and groups and communities of all kinds.

What does theology look like when it grows up in a refugee settlement, in a resident group of Germans and foreign workers, among the handicapped, in the context of labor conflicts among trade unions? In my opinion it is a pity that our theological schools modeled themselves so closely on the university faculties instead of developing their own forms of theology (though in truth they were driven to it by our problematic examination system).

A further conclusion: It is no longer possible to do scientific theology in isolation from other disciplines. Theological work was always carried on in an interdisciplinary context: historical disciplines were grouped with the corresponding historical sciences, systematic theology with philosophy, and practical theology, at least in recent times, with the humane sciences. These must now, however, become the partners also of the systematic and historical disciplines, and that not only by taking cognizance of literary productions but by lively interaction in research and doctrine. After the far too small beginnings which I have experienced as a theologian in a special department of philosophy and social sciences which had learned to look on this as its task, I cannot now be very hopeful about theological work outside such an interdisciplinary context.

Finally, the work within the theological faculty. If theology, according to the old tradition, sees itself as *scientia practica* arising from practice with a view to practice, that places practical theology today in the midst of a community of theological works. It is not only, as it was for Schleiermacher, the "crown of theological study," for this might indicate only a decorative function; it must, rather, be the heart of theology. Under the suggestion of the modern concept of science, to which the theological faculties have proved compliant, theology accepted the role of a Cinderella from which it has not yet freed itself. If Christian theology is to understand itself aright, then in its heart it is practical theology. Practical theology, therefore, is the heart of a theological faculty, and the other theological disciplines work along with it as auxiliary disciplines.

RECOMMENDED READING

Brecht, Bertolt. *Der Tui* (novel). In *Gesammelte Werke,* Vol. 12; *Gesammelte Prosa,* Vol. 2.

Cardenal, Ernesto. *Das Evangelium der Bauern von Solentiname.* 2 vols. 1976, 1978.

Casalis, George. *Les Idées justes ne tombent pas du ciel.* 1977. (German: *Die richtigen Ideen fallen nicht vom Himmel herab.* 1978.)

Castillo, Fernando (ed.). *Theologie aus der Praxis des Volkes.* Neuere Studien zum lateinamerikanischen Christentum und zur Theologie der Befreiung. 1978.

Gutiérrez, Gustavo. *Theologie der Befreiung.* 1973.

Spiegel, Yorick. *Kirche und Klassenbindung.* Editions Suhrkamp, No. 709.

III   The Bible

*What constitutes the significance and indispensability
of the Bible for Christian faith, and consequently also
for theology? Modern science has made untenable earlier conceptions of the historical reliability and unity of
the Bible. At the same time, this has not reduced the
significance of the Bible. This throws light upon the way
in which theology today relates itself to the Bible.*

The ultimate authority for Christian faith, and thus also
for Christian theology, is the Bible, the Old Testament
and the New. It is a collection of human writings. Are
some people in consequence given an ultimate authority
over others, an extreme form of heteronomy, a faith in
authority, which makes Christianity unacceptable to autonomous reason—and is this not a tautology? Can reason
be anything but autonomous? This objection has been
voiced since the beginning of the modern age. The
theologian speaks "according to statutory prescriptions
for belief, which are contained in a book, preferably
called the Bible, that is, in a codex containing the
revelation of an old and a new covenant, . . . which was
established many hundreds of years ago." Also: "That a
God exists is proved by the biblical theologian from the
fact that he has spoken in the Bible." So wrote Immanuel
Kant in his book *Der Streit der Fakultäten* (The conflict
of faculties),[22] and in the same strain Wilhelm Weischedel writes today:

> The believer submits himself to an authority both at
> the beginning and in the continuing act of faith. He
> knows and acknowledges one final truth beyond
> questioning, one unconditional authority. In visible

46

form, that is the church, or the word of Scripture. In a deeper sense it is the Lordship of God mediated by Jesus Christ, to which the believer unreservedly commits himself. The philosopher, on the other hand, would betray his cause if he were to acknowledge another authority than his own thinking and the reality which he perceives in the act of thought. This means, however, that philosophical thought functions in freedom.[23]

We must accordingly develop our reflections about the constraint and freedom of theological thinking in relation to the significance of the Bible, inasmuch as we do not wish to remain saddled with this alternative: theology=unfree thinking, philosophy=free thinking (and only as such deserving its name)—an alternative that would be intolerable for evangelical theology at least, for a theology of the "freedom of a Christian man."

The suggestion that evangelical theology is subject to a heteronomous court of appeal with final authority is made plausible by the fact of the establishment of the Reformation four hundred years ago on the Bible. Luther proclaimed the principle *sola scriptura* ("Scripture alone"), and the Lutheran confessions taught that Holy Scripture must be *judex, norma et regula* ("judge, norm, and rule") in the church and for the church.[24] Thus, at all events, a unique significance of the Bible for the Christian faith is claimed. What makes the Bible so important?

In the first place we must remember that the principle *sola scriptura* was actually a rejection of all final, absolute authority exercised over men by men, and consequently an act of *liberation*. Against the ascription of absolute authority to a human tribunal—that of the pope, and consequently of the episcopal councils—this proclamation was meant to ensure that in the church, and consequently also in the world, no one can exercise a total lordship over others and that no priestly caste possessing arcane knowledge can subject the life and thought of other persons to itself. The place of the highest and final authority, which therefore both establishes and calls into question all human authority, must remain free! No human authority may identify itself with it. Thus the principle *sola scriptura* had and has primarily significance as a criticism of authority and a safeguard of freedom.

Therefore Luther translated the Bible, and put it in the hands of the people, in order that everyone might come of age, might judge (and pass judgment even on the highest human authorities) and have a voice. *Sola scriptura* and the "universal priesthood of all believers" belong together. Expressed in modern concepts, this means a declaration that the church is not hierarchical but democratic.

In their day, at a time of profound crisis in social authority, Luther and the Reformers reestablished, first, authority in the church, and then social authority. They did not establish it as the independent authority of a highest organ of the church over the church, but through subjecting the church to Holy Scripture: insofar as the church acts "according to Scripture" it participates in the authority of Scripture. On this point the young Karl Marx expressed the suspicion that it means only the exchange of an outward subjection (to the teaching office of the church) for an inward, much more effective, subjection:

> Luther certainly abolished a slavery of *devotion*, because he put in its place a slavery motivated by *conviction*. He broke the faith in authority, because he restored the authority of faith. He turned the priests into laymen, because he turned the laymen into priests. He freed men from external religiosity because he made religiosity the inner man. He set free the body from its chain, because he enchained the heart.[25]

This reproach is not peculiar to the Marxian critique of religion. While the theology of German idealism celebrated this interiorization of religiosity, as the decisive liberating achievement of the Reformation, there has always been, in modern times, an accompanying call for a second Reformation, which should complete the first Reformation by also loosing the ties that bind it to the "paper pope" of the Bible, and thus in a consistent manner restore man's independence of human domination.

But today the question is not only whether the acknowledgment of the authority of the Bible is to be regarded as good or bad, as a total or only a partial emancipation. The additional question has been raised as to whether the Bible, as it is now understood, is at all capable of acting as an authority for church and theology, if it can in fact function as *unica norma et judex*. For this presupposes (1) that the Bible speaks unambiguously with *one* voice, as it is a condition for a norm or a judge that they should be consistent with themselves, and (2) that this one voice, even if it can be heard only through the medium of men ("apostles and prophets"), should be audible as the voice of the one living God. Both these conditions were secured in the tradition of the church, and were supported by the doctrine of the inspiration of the biblical writers by the Holy Spirit, in appearance most consistently by the doctrine of verbal inspiration, i.e., the inspiration of every word, nay, every letter of the Bible, a doctrine developed by the old Protestant theology of the sixteenth to the eighteenth century to serve as a support of the *"sola scriptura"* of the Reformers. Here, by "God's word" is to be understood a decree dictated by God, to which man has to subject himself unconditionally, comparable with the order to attack given by a divisional commander, to be understood, and to be obeyed, literally.

From the standpoint of freedom and faith, Catholicism and Protestantism in this matter come out equally badly. For if, as we must later make clear to ourselves, we understand faith in the strictly biblical sense (and here, indeed, we can speak of a unity which is maintained with few exceptions throughout the biblical writings) as personal trust in God, then it follows that such faith in God would have to be preceded by the fulfillment of a condition, fulfillment of a work to be performed by me— namely, the act of submission to a human authority, either that of the church's teaching office (the pope) or that of the biblical authors. First would come the act of faith as an assent to the truth of authority and the statements of this authority, and only then, as a result, the act of faith as trust in the promises of God.

Of course in such a case use is made of the assertion, which every human power has clutched at when it wishes to secure the total subjection of people, that it was instituted and inspired by God, was sent by Providence (Hitler) or was the conscious implement of the law of historical development ("The Party is always right"). But this is precisely what is forbidden in the first commandment of the Decalogue. "You shall have no other gods before me" sets its face against the idolizing of every human authority. Thus by such identification of the Bible with God's word, by such investing of the Bible with divine authority, by laying down the previous condition of a work to be performed by us ("Bible faith," as one can often hear it called even today in religious circles) as coming *before* trust in God's word addressed to us, we involve ourselves in hopeless contradiction with what the Bible itself has to tell us about the nature of faith.

Therefore it is good, in a Christian sense, that this theory of verbal inspiration has been destroyed by modern science. This is an example of how wrong it is to reject *en bloc* scientific thought, or even modern thought in general, in the name of faith, because it has so often expressed and expresses itself in anti-Christian or even atheist terms, as if for that reason it could not still have its truth and be an instrument of God. But to hold just such a belief must be possible to Christian faith, if it takes seriously its confession that God rules the world.

Modern biblical research has treated the Bible as a human book, as a historical document (the method of historical criticism). The result is that, as far as the historicity of the biblical statements is concerned, they are a mixture of historical correctness and error; its utterances were stamped by the contemporary world view and state of knowledge, and also by the contemporary conditions of society. In addition, they are in many ways related to the religious world environment, both in adopting some of its elements and in repudiating them (method of comparative religion). Within the Bible—and that means within the thousand years in which the Old Testament took shape, and within the eighty years or so in which the New Testament took shape—a development occurs in which earlier conceptions disappear, or are changed, or are replaced by newer ones, and sometimes come to life again. And in conclusion, alongside the differences between the conceptions that result from this development, there are also differences between the conceptions of the individual biblical authors, even when they are living at the same time; so that, over and above the contradictions in the Bible which men noticed in earlier times and tried hard to reconcile with the doctrine of verbal inspiration, we can perceive much deeper contradictions in both Testaments, and also between the two Testaments. From this comes the necessity of a theological criticism of content, which tests the individual biblical writings to see how far they are coherent with themselves, and whether, and how far, they are in irreconcilable contradiction with other scriptural writings and utterances.

Thus the Bible is, as it now appears, not a unity, but a small library and it contains many different and divergent voices. It consists of thirty-nine books in the Old Testament, twenty-seven in the New Testament, and in addition fourteen books or writings in the Old Testament Apocrypha which in Catholicism are given an equal status with the rest of the biblical writings. The person who still speaks of *the* Bible, and *the* Holy Scriptures, seems to be hopelessly out of date, and the Bible can no longer be called "the word of God," because its human character and historical conditioning is obvious, and because a voice of God which is broken up into so many divergent voices does not help us, but makes us perplexed. This was evident even in past days from the fact that—apparently—anything can be proved from the Bible, the Jews against the Christians, and vice versa, and in like manner the Christian confessions and groups against each other.

The Bible is the literary deposit of a tradition more than one thousand years old, diverse, and undergoing continuous historical change. For this reason it appears that we can no longer—with the Reformers and in opposition to Rome—confront church tradition with Holy Scripture as a critical principle; and for this reason—apparently—only a living teaching office could help us, an office with higher authority than the whole of tradition, including the Bible as a part thereof. It could help us to preach the gospel authoritatively, to be sure of its content, and to believe with certainty. And it could help us to protect the unity of the church from the fragmentation caused by divergent interpretations of the Bible. Such a teaching office, equipped with immediate divine inspiration, would decide what in this whole tradition is divine, what comes from God and is therefore binding.

So it is understandable that for a long time there was strong opposition in the Christian churches to the disintegration of biblical unity and authority by historical research, and it is equally understandable that the views of the Bible held by the form-historical school led the Catholic side to a short-lived triumph, since, thanks to the living papal teaching office, it seemed to be less damaged by these views. All the more honor to Protestantism, in my opinion, that in it free scientific investigation of the Bible (with the exception of some fundamentalist groups) won the day earlier than in Catholicism, where it has been allowed free scope only in the last twenty years or so—a significant ecumenical event.

I have said several times "as it appears." How can we lose our fear of historical research? How can the Bible, in spite of the disintegration of its former authoritative form, retain its importance for church and faith? As a matter of fact, that is what has happened. In the worship of God, in arguments with each other about questions of the Christian life, as a book of congregational and individual edification, strengthening, and instruction, as the basic text of all Christian theology—at no point has the Bible played its last card; its unique significance is continually demonstrated in action.

Is this schizophrenia? Are these merely the persistent aftereffects of its earlier prestige, now dead and buried, without this burial having been acknowledged in practice? Or, for those who no longer resist the historicocritical view of the Bible, what in spite of all makes the Bible still important, indispensable, and authoritative? Württemberg curates in 1970 blithely declared that the Bible was for them merely one book among others, from which they could draw impulses for their thought and action today exactly as from other books. There was indignation over this. But are the church authorities to say to them, "First you must give the Bible a special place, and only then can you be ministers"? Or can the church dare to say to them: "Good, the chief thing is that *beside* the other voices you should really listen attentively to the voices that speak to us through the Bible, and ask for their possible significance today, then all will be well. For then indeed the voice of the Bible will unmistakably make itself heard, and take precedence over the other voices, and become the standard by which they are judged. But if it does not thrust back the other voices into the second place, it will itself be thrust back, and that will indeed have far-reaching results for you. For then you will become servants of other gospels, and useless for the service of Christian proclamation. It will not, as a matter of fact, be possible for you in the long run to hear the Bible and take it seriously *alongside* other books; it thrusts itself forward and upward—or it is thrust down. And we shall all have to be patient and take that risk."

In fact, that is the only way—and it is precisely the same as the way in which the Bible came to have significance both in Judaism and in Christianity. This did not happen because someone stood up and declared, "Here is a book that has fallen from heaven; you must bow down before it!" What happened was that the Bible "imposed itself," as Karl Barth expressed it; it carried the day by its own worth, and made itself the canon and yardstick of all who were not concerned to invent a religion or a Christianity for themselves, but to pass on this special message of God authentically in the same way as it had come to them.

But what is the relation of the Bible to this message? And how could I permit myself several times to speak of the Bible as if it were a single voice and not a conglomerate of different voices? The two questions are closely connected.

Historical research has not completed its work when it has sharply distinguished and discriminated between the individual voices which find expression in this library. It must also ask what brings these voices together, whether possibly there is a unity in which they are combined, and in consequence of which it was possible for them to be heard together in unison and distinguished from other contemporary voices, as in fact happened. These writings are already united by the fact that they come from the same community of faith, Israel and the church; that, in spite of their conceptual differences, they all refer us to the same center, the God of Israel and the Christ event; and that they were recognized by their community of faith as a correct representation of their faith, and consequently became the standard by which the other voices that found expression in their community were judged.

Since we are no longer prejudiced by taboo, and by the formal postulate of unity, we must now establish whether a unity of content is to be found in the biblical writings, a common trend, a unity deriving from their object, a common exemplarity and authenticity in their language about it, and one that transcends the many differences among them. This was never taken for granted. There have always been "antilegomena," i.e., writings whose legitimate place in the canon was disputed. But on essentials there have been sufficient positive arguments wherever people joined together in fellowship to hear the Bible and to take it seriously as it was handed down from generation to generation.

Today also this becomes evident, now that Catholic and Protestant exegetes and Christians of various denominations, and of late Christians and Jews, have begun studying the Bible together, and now that the Catholic exegetes are no longer subject to the prejudgments of their teaching office but are free to seek the meaning of the text, reading the Bible and studying it like any other book. It is this which sets the Bible free and releases its power to bring us together, making it the greatest influence in favor of ecumenical unity.

Admittedly it has this unitive power when, and only when, we do *not*, as has often happened, expect of it a unity like that of a dogmatic system—a legal code, or a list of axioms—which could serve as the basis for a system without contradictions, constructed with mathematical logic, or for an ideological party program. Anyone who requires that, and understands only such a unity, understands the church also as a party, and the doctrine of the church as a philosophical or mathematical system. But the unity of the church is of another order, and so is the unity of the Bible. We must represent it to ourselves in the same way as we ourselves experience it in the church.

We experience the *church* when we find ourselves in a circle of people who have been mobilized and brought together by the message of Christ, and exchange views about what they have heard and about what is to be done now. There will be no lack of strong communal feeling, nor will the difference of individual viewpoints be missing. There will be the mixture of non-Christian elements which have not yet been purged away, and which need correction. There will be a difference of accents—conflicts of character and interests, age gaps, and the tensions resulting from all these causes. The case is exactly similar when we enter the circle of the biblical authors. And just as the variety and the contradictions within the living circle of the disciples of Jesus do not prevent a person who enters it, and who through it hears the message of Christ, from coming to faith and discipleship by means of this hearing, no more does this manifold and contradictory character and individuality of the circle of the biblical witnesses to God—the "cloud of witnesses" (Heb. 12:1)—prevent their common message from getting through.

Let us set forth these reflections under several headings:

1. The indispensability of the Bible is based on the historical character of its message. This message brings us today into contact with the one to whom it bears witness by the telling of his already completed actions and his promises and instructions already given.

2. The fellowship of faith was built up through experiencing these actions and through hearing the claim which they make. From among the voices which were heard within it, and which gave expression to these experiences, it has chosen those voices which seemed to it most authentic, in order to make them the standards by which to judge all other voices and testimonies of experience that find expression in this fellowship and within its ambience.

3. This selection is one made by a human fellowship. This means:

a. It has in its favor that *these* voices thus impressed themselves upon this fellowship, and that they have made possible the transmission of the message, and the critical sifting of this transmission, again and again, up to the present day.

b. The selection includes passages which, because of their concentrated witness, are outstanding in their significances, some that are called into question, and many, too, that will always remain disputed.

4. That to which witness is borne—or, better, the one to whom witness is borne—is not directly identical with any of these witnesses. His word, i.e., what he has to say to us, is not above or behind these witnesses, but is to be heard in them and through them. In this hearing there occurs a separation (it is not made by us, but occurs of itself), between the human instrument and the divine word. The case is exactly similar to the hearing of a sermon today, or any other witness borne to Jesus Christ

and the God of Abraham, Isaac, and Jacob. The divine word addresses us unconditionally, and binds us unconditionally to itself; the human word, being human, is subject to our criticism.

5. What Luther says of the psalms (in his Introduction to the Psalter, 1531) holds good of the whole Bible: "There you see into the heart of all the saints." The humanity of the biblical authors is not extinguished or concealed, but is actually exposed. This has far-reaching consequences for our relationship to the Bible:

a. It owes its reputation, its canonical validity, to its concentration on its matter, on the message imparted to the fellowship whose voices speak to us here, *and* to the proximity in time of its authors (especially the New Testament authors) to the divine actions which they attest. By this they are distinguished from all later authors. Karl Barth[26] calls this their "direct confrontation" with their object, and means thereby both their proximity in time and the direct relation in which prophets and apostles stood to their divine taskmaster and to the man Jesus Christ. We must consider, in addition, as we said, the experience of the church with just these writings, an experience that rests upon this direct confrontation and confirms it by its selection of them for the canon. For this reason, as Barth says,[27] as "witnesses of the first order" they have an inalienable advantage over us, the "witnesses of the second order," and are to be, first, last, and always, consulted as the first reliable experts in the matter we are considering.

b. The historical character of these "witnesses of the first order" makes necessary the *trans-lation* of their witness into the present. This can happen only if we take their historical character seriously, i.e., by means of an interpretation that seeks first to understand at a historical distance what they had then, in their time and place, to say to their hearers and not to us. Since historical work has been predominantly concerned with the history of ideas, today its supplementation—hitherto largely neglected—by a historico-materialist method of exegesis, i.e., an exegesis that employs the historico-materialist method of questioning history, is rightly demanded. This draws into sharper profile the historical character of the authors: they speak as conditioned by the social circumstances and conflicting interests of their time; they are stamped, limited, and challenged by them, and they relate the message critically, or accommodate it to the conditions of their time. The individualizing tendency of an exegesis that overlooks this, or regards it as marginal, corresponds to an individualistic understanding of the gospel in which feudal and bourgeois class society has an interest, and does not allow scope for the sociocritical dimension of the Bible. This, however, is of importance for the second stage of trans-lation: what can things said at that time signify today for us and in relation to our time, in our very different circumstances? For this reason we cannot stop at recitation and historical understanding; actualization is necessary, and it can only happen if now, having listened attentively, we say on our own responsibility "not similar things, but the same thing." I would like to call this the prophetic dimension of biblical interpretation.

c. Both the historical difference and the human character, as well as the human limitation and fallibility, of the "witnesses of the first order" leave us, though bound to them, also free from them. We do not believe in the Bible, and it is not for us God's word bound between the two covers of a book. Such an understanding of it would result in a legalistic relation to it that would contradict the evangelical freedom to which it bears witness, and which also finds expression in the individual particularity of their voices. Luther coined the famous formula for this, that not everything in the Bible is equally important and binding for us, but that we should seek for "what deals with Christ," i.e., for what is intended as "glad tidings" of God's reality and kingdom in the individual biblical utterances. Luther does not mean a lexicographical listing of the passages where Jesus Christ is mentioned, but an inquiry directed to every section of the Bible (even in the Old Testament!) to see whether, and in how far, it causes us to perceive a relation to what is revealed in the Christ event. This inquiry must not be omitted even in the apparently driest, least Christ-centered, most irrelevant pages of the Bible. The distinctions and decisions to which it leads (i.e., its positive or negative results) are, in the first place, our own; we are responsible for them, and perhaps they are caused by limitations in our individual outlook. The church must give us the freedom to express our negative judgments, i.e., to use "detective biblical criticism,"[28] to point out, even in biblical texts, an accommodation to class interests, which serves to soften the radical character of the original message, and which for that reason must be exposed and corrected in our exposition. At the same time, we must give the church the freedom not to accept our results without question and make them obligatory, but rather to leave the texts criticized by us in the canon. This gives the texts the chance to say to us how far they in their day, if so modified, could truly have conveyed the full import of the message. Thus all our doubts about a biblical text do not constitute a final judgment about it; they leave it the freedom to speak to others in a manner different from the way it speaks to us, and they leave others the freedom to find other things than we have succeeded in finding. Thus it is precisely the nonidentity of the Bible and God's word that protects the freedom of God and our human freedom.

For this reason the first thesis of the Barmen Declaration of the Confessing Church of 1934 brings the Bible and God's word into a positive connection, but without identification. It is not the Bible that is God's word; rather, "Jesus Christ as he is attested to us in Holy Scripture is the one word of God, whom we are to hear, whom we are to trust in life and in death, and whom we are to obey."[29]

RECOMMENDED READING

Barth, Markus. "Vom Geheimnis der Bibel." In *Theologische Existenz heute*, No. 100. 1962.

Kähler, Martin. *Aufsätze zur Bibelfrage*, edited by Ernst Kähler. Theologische Bücherei, No. 37. 1967.

Käsemann, Ernst. *Der Ruf der Freiheit.* 1968.

Käsemann, Ernst (ed.). *Das Neue Testament als Kanon.* 1970.

Miskotte, Kornelis Heiko. *Wenn die Götter schweigen. Vom Sinn des alten Testaments.* 1963.

IV   Jesus Christ

*In the center of the Christian faith, and consequently
the center also of theological reflection, there stand the
event of Jesus Christ and the extraordinary statements
that the New Testament writings have made about his
universal significance. The humanity of Jesus, and his
specific humanity as a Jew, is just as much to be taken in
earnest as the absolute character of these claims regarding his significance. The latter have their center in the
New Testament words "for us," which signify the self-
identification of the eternal God with this concrete
human being for the salvation of his human race, in
order to bring about the realization of the Kingdom of
God.*

Christian Theology Serves the Christian Church

The adjective "Christian" comes from Jesus Christ. We
cannot emphasize this strongly enough—we who misuse
this adjective so carelessly and link it with culture, the
West, political parties, and even marriage bureaus!

Christian theology reflects on the Christian message.
That is the message of the two parts of the Bible, which
are heard together, belong together, and are handed
down together by the Christian church: the Hebrew
Bible (the Old Testament) and its primitive Christian
continuation, the New Testament. The whole of this
Bible is the fundamental witness concerning those experiences and that event from which the church took its
origin and whose message it has to pass on. The event
that binds together the two parts of the Bible, the two
Testaments, bears the name of a man, Jesus of Nazareth,
and the description reserved for this man, which now

distinguishes him from all other men: this Jesus is *the* Christ, *the* Messiah = *the* Anointed of the God of Abraham, Isaac, and Jacob, of the God of Israel. Anyone who concerns himself with Christian theology is centrally concerned with this event. *Nil nisi Christum praedicare* ("to proclaim nothing but Christ") was described by Luther as *the* task of the Christian church.[30] This is the only ground for applying to it the adjective "Christian."

Our purpose here cannot be to trace the outlines of a Christology. Only some fundamental questions will be dealt with, questions that arise for everyone who applies himself to the phenomenon of the central place of Jesus Christ in Christian faith, and for the Christian church, whether he stands within it or inquires from without:

1. Who is it that occupies this central position?
2. Of what does this central position consist?

1. Who is it that occupies this central position?

a. It is a man. *Vere homo,* truly a man, says the Christian creed. This at once directs our gaze to a concrete historical man, and warns us against the dangers of docetism, i.e., a kind of thinking that starts with a Christ idea, a form built up out of dogmatic concepts, and only then, subsequently, comes to speak of this man, as if he were merely the historical exemplification or illustration of such an idea.

In the center stands a single, real man, with a human destiny, "born of a woman" (Gal. 4:4), historically conditioned and limited like every man, belonging to a particular people, age, and cultural context, mortal, capable of error like all of us. This presupposes that the historical question of whether there ever was such a man, which from the nineteenth century to the beginning of the twentieth century was violently discussed, is today settled, i.e., answered historically in the affirmative. It is, however, significant for the Christian faith that at its center stands a man whose historical existence, like that of every other man, can be historically doubted; this heel of Achilles, this dubitability, is essential to Christianity, it stands and falls with the problematical historical existence of this man, and it actually makes its boast of this as the real historical act of God, through which the eternal, invisible God savingly interposed in the history of humanity.

This brings us to our first fundamental question. How can such a particular event have universal significance—significance, that is, for all human beings, for the whole of human history, or perhaps even over and above this, for the whole universe, the whole cosmos? Has this perhaps to do with the singular teaching of Jesus? Every teaching is singular, because every individual is singular. But every teaching is both capable of improvement, and needs improvement, and bears the marks of its temporal conditioning. We cannot subject ourselves blindly to any teaching.

The view of the Christian church is as follows: What Jesus taught in his life is also worthy to be heard in all ages. But the reason for this is that he is in his *person* unique, because with his life and destiny he is an event of universal significance.

b. Jesus is a *Jewish* man. "Jesus Christ would not be what he is if he were not the Christ, the bearer of office, who comes out of *Israel*, who is the *Jew* Jesus."[31] The Jewishness of Jesus does not merely signify an accidental piece of information, i.e., that he belonged like every one of us to a particular people, but by accident to the Jewish people at a definite time. The meaning is, rather, that Jesus stands, with his teaching *and* what happened to him and through him, as its central event, in an indissoluble, and for him, as its central event, essential, connection with the peculiar character of precisely *this* people, with that which this people has heard, experienced, believed, lived, and hoped from its beginning to this day. It is only an apparent contradiction of the universal significance of Jesus that precisely in his case the bond with this people is closer, his belonging to just this people is more important than that of the other great figures of history with international significance. True, in their case too, their belonging to a people is not unimportant; it belongs to things that condition their individuality. But though they also belong irretrievably to their people and their time, we may even disregard their nationality. Luther's statement, "I was born among my Germans, I will serve them,"[32] expressed an honorable moral principle, but if he had been compelled to emigrate, it could have hindered him from taking another people as collective of reference for his service. Of an entirely different quality is the word of Jesus: "I was sent only to the lost sheep of the house of Israel" (Matt. 15:24). Jesus belongs in the first place *not* to the whole of humanity, but in the first place to this people of his (Rom. 1:16). He is in the first place an event within Judaism, and is not merely accidentally but essentially connected with Jewish history and the most important elements of its singularity: covenant, election, law, prophecy, land, uniqueness of the God of Israel, messianic expectation. On every page of the New Testament this bond of connection between Jesus and the history of the Jewish people is mentioned in one way or another, and behind this stands the claim of the central significance of this one Jew for all Jews, for the whole Jewish people. The centrality of Christ for the whole of humanity, which the New Testament asserts, grows out of the centrality of Jesus for Israel. For this reason the New Testament cannot be separated from the Hebrew Bible. But for this reason it is impossible to speak in Christian terms of the centrality of Jesus without at the same time speaking of a central function of the Jewish people for the whole of humanity. That is the second striking point about the confession by Christian faith of Jesus as Christ.

c. This significance of the real historical Jewish man Jesus of Nazareth makes a third matter even more striking: our historically assured knowledge of just this man is slight—so slight that, as has been said, it has been possible to doubt even his historical existence. David Friedrich Strauss once observed that our knowledge of the historical Socrates is greater than our knowledge of the historical Jesus, yet Socrates left behind him nothing written by his hand. The cause of this is not that Athens was culturally more developed than Jerusalem, for from early days Judaism was extraordinarily capable of passing on tradition; nor was it because Socrates had such highly educated scholars and handers down of tradition as Plato and Xenophon, while among the disciples, in contrast, the intellectual sector of contemporary Judaism was lacking, and was only to be represented after Easter by Paul and the evangelists. But this lack, together with the absence of historical witnesses outside the disciples' circle, is all the more striking because Jesus' life was one that was not inconspicuous, nor was it passed in secluded quiet. The last part of his life at least, the strikingly short time of his activity as a public speaker and healer, was spent in the glare of publicity, and it moved his people profoundly and gathered a strong movement around him.

In view of this, it is understandable that the question could be raised whether the earthly life of Jesus has any significance at all for Christian faith, and whether indeed it was only the hopes which the new community attached to his person after Easter (a subject to which we must turn at once) that have significance for us, so that the significance of his life is limited to the naked *fact* of his existence and its fatal conclusion (Rudolf Bultmann).[33] In the same way the question could be raised as to whether the man who, after Easter, thought the significance of this fact through with the greatest detail and penetration and interpreted it, and who beyond this fact of the cross tells almost nothing of Jesus' life, namely Paul, was not the true founder of Christianity; in comparison with Paul therefore, the narratives about the life of Jesus in the Gospels were dispensable.

Against this, the post-Easter community of the church was by no means of this opinion, but handed down much material about Jesus' words and actions. It did not attach its faith, with all its statements about Christ, to Jesus as to an authority void of content. Nor did it ascribe to him a significance that had no basis in his life, but said expressly that it had derived this significance from his life. Its faith in Christ is unthinkable without the material supplied to it by Jesus' life.

It saw all this in a new light because of Easter and because of new events which had the effect on it of divine disclosures of the Spirit. Its accounts of Jesus were thereby given a new color, and repeatedly given a new form as well. In the Gospels words of Jesus are also preserved which were obviously no longer correctly understood by the later writers, or could no longer be accepted in their original sense, and for that reason were given a new interpretation (just as, for that matter also continued to happen in the later history of exegesis of such words in the course of church history!). This fact indicates that the Jesus tradition of the fellowship was, not a new creation, but the handing down of previously given material, a store containing the things that contemporaries of Jesus had seen and experienced.

Further, this store of pre-Easter experiences of Jesus was only passed on to the fellowship after Easter by those who had attached themselves to Jesus, and it was not felt necessary to amplify and confirm this by the neutral reports of other eyewitnesses outside the circle of Jesus' disciples. The reason for this was not only that in those days our modern historical sense, which insists upon the greatest possible objectivity and demonstrability of a report, had not yet developed. That is true, but it is not the whole truth. For in the ancient world there did exist a historiography which—even if not in our strictly critical manner—attempted to tell "what really happened" (Leopold von Ranke). And Luke in his preface states his intention of "writing an orderly account" of the events that had happened, "that you may know the truth concerning those things of which you have been informed" (Luke 1:3f.). But even so, Luke's Gospel, like the other Gospels, is unlike the writing of the ancient historians. The Gospels are something unique in ancient literature, veritably the creation of a new form of literature, and, like the letters of Paul, which are unique in the epistolary literature of the ancient world, they are a sign of the novelty of the phenomenon which had come into the midst of the ancient world and among the Jewish people. They hand down a given store of narratives which is based on things that really happened. Yet they do so in such a way that, because of the new interpretation placed upon the given material, the material itself can no longer be sifted out to result in a historically reliable picture of the "historical Jesus." As Albert Schweitzer has shown, this attempt to investigate the life of Jesus has miscarried. It resulted in a multitude of Jesus novels dressed up as historical biographies of Jesus. Even our newer books about Jesus (down to the one by David Flusser, which is designed with critical awareness), relying sometimes more and sometimes less on the historical reliability of the Synoptic writers, have the merit of bringing us nearer to the historical Jesus, but they do not disprove Adolf von Harnack's licentiate thesis: *Vita Christi scribi nequit* ("The life of Christ cannot be written").

What can be concluded from this very striking fact? As

we said, this points neither to the insignificance of the earthly life of Jesus nor to the hope of finally achieving an objective historical picture of Jesus by the use of still subtler methods and new sources.

But the situation ought not to be other than it is! Jesus does not objectify himself in any way, either by leaving behind him written records which would ensure that his disciples' preaching was authentic, or by means of a formulated doctrine as in a catechism, or institutionally, e.g., by rites (Baptism and the Lord's Supper) or by setting up authorities and organizations. Even the circle of disciples he gathered has no sharp boundaries, and the calling of twelve, if we assume that this circle was formed by Jesus himself, is only an indication of his claim to the whole of Israel, not an arrangement intended to be permanent. Only one prayer, the Lord's Prayer, is taught by him as a formula to be observed, and even this is a composition taken from the prayer tradition of the Jews. As he did in his life, so in later days he withdraws himself from all objectification.

Or does he? As a mortal man he can be objectified like each of us, for which reason he is a legitimate object of historical inquiry. But as the eschatological speaker and utterance of God he cannot be objectified, he cannot be contemplated with indifference; he finds the man whom he finds; to meet him is a decision, through which it is revealed who one is (John 3:18–21); it is a judgment, and at the same time the turning point of life. No one can be neutral in relation to him; indeed, to attempt to be neutral is to close oneself off from him. The knowledge and acknowledgment of him is based, not on objective experiment, but on inner revelation, not through "flesh and blood" (Matt. 16:17). "No one knows the Son except the Father, and no one knows the Father except the Son and any one to whom the Son chooses to reveal him" (Matt. 11:27). The paradox is exactly expressed in John

1:14. As one who has "become flesh" he can be made an object, the theme of historical inquiry, but *who* he really is, *what* happens when he comes on the scene, cannot be assessed in objective terms. What he says and does can be seen and heard, but in its totality it is a sign corresponding to a reality that can only be known in a nonobjective manner through the discipleship of faith. It is a sign that remains an enigma, with its contradiction between the highest claim and the deepest humility, between binding to itself and pointing away from itself, between having extraordinary power and yet coming to a pitiful end. It is a riddle that remains a riddle so long as it is not seen in the light of *that* knowledge of faith which finds expression in the Christological confession of faith. In that confession the contradictions are fused together, they fall into unison. To the man who takes discipleship on himself the truth will become visible through the paradox. But discipleship means that this knowledge cannot be had without its consequences. If man allows himself to be drawn into the consequences, to him Jesus becomes the central figure of the world, to whom there is no equal, and *beside* whom there is no other; this means that Jesus is so united with the God of Israel that as no one can stand beside this God, so no one can stand beside him. Thus Jesus participates in the God of Israel who sent him, who also cannot be objectified or observed, who therefore also cannot be possessed or put at our disposal, of whom instead Martin Buber's word holds good: "The Eternal Thou, in the nature of things, cannot become an It."[34]

2. Of what does this central position of Jesus Christ consist?

As we have seen, the centrality of Jesus in the Christian faith is intimately connected with the centrality of Israel's God for Israel, which had already become for

Israel a centrality for the whole world. The togetherness of Jesus with the God of Israel is later expounded in ancient church dogma in a very dialectical manner, as a unity of identity in nonidentity, and certainly it grew out of the exceptional manner in which Jesus came forward "in the name of God." It is thus to be understood first from a viewpoint *internal* to the Jewish people.

From this viewpoint it is what no Jew may claim for himself, or allow to another, because of the "infinite qualitative difference between God and man" (Kierkegaard)—a difference that in Israel far transcended Greek monotheism, and was conceived of as a practical reminder to man of his status, and confronts every philosophy of identity with its strict line of demarcation between Creator and creature. On the other hand, it did *not* signify for those Jews who followed Jesus a declension into heathenish deification of the creature, nor a declension into the identity thinking of Greek or Asiatic religion. It was, on the contrary, conceived as the most amazing, incredibly radical embodiment of the loyalty of the covenant God to his people (and thus to the humanity implicated in his election). In Jesus of Nazareth there takes place the identification of the God of Israel with his people, and with humanity, with all the consequences that follow.

a. God's identification, in Jesus, with his people and with humanity takes place with all the consequences *for himself.*

It is no longer possible to reckon with a God far away from man who, in unmoved and immovable apathy, sits enthroned above us, a stranger to the sufferings of his creation. When, in the word of the Old Testament prophet, this God suffers at the hands of his people; when, according to Isaiah 53, the servant of the Lord takes vicariously the sufferings and guilt of the people upon himself—that then is, as the New Testament authors see, a prophecy which becomes massive and concrete reality. In this Jesus, and identifying himself with him, the exalted and eternal God, whose transcendence Israel conceives in far more radical terms than did the Greek philosophers, becomes the suffering God, the one abandoned in weakness. To him nothing human is any longer alien—except sin, says Heb. 4:15. There is no longer any human life and human suffering that is alien to this God, not even death, and the man who asks why God permits our sufferings must now take seriously the fact that this God in the first place allows the sufferings of man to afflict himself. The man who seeks this God in his own sufferings finds him now as the one at his side, in his suffering, and is pointed now, not to heaven, but to an appalling place of suffering on this earth. Here God is truly "wholly other" than men have otherwise thought him to be, and are accustomed to think him. The question then arises, how does it help us that now even God is drawn into suffering, and is that not the end of all our hope in a God who, thanks to his superiority over suffering, and even over all human guilt, could help us? This question is answered by means of the inexhaustible "for us" which is the chief theme of Paul, above all. This leads us to the second aspect.

b. God's identification, in Jesus, with his people and with humanity takes place with all the consequences for this one man, *for Jesus.*

Jesus is the "elect" man, chosen for this act of self-identification and solidarity of the God of Israel with Israel, *and* consequently with the whole of humanity. This makes his life and his suffering an event "for us" in a quite different, much more universal sense than anything that we can do and suffer for each other—namely, for all men everywhere. This "for us" is the central expression for an understanding of the destiny of Jesus which was given to primitive Christianity and which is carried out into the world. There is scarcely anything more surprising in the spiritual life of mankind than the opening up of this new insight immediately after the dreadful end of Jesus by a death of torment on the cross. It could neither have been foreseen nor shown rationally to be necessary; it transcends even the thoughts that were already current in Judaism concerning the representative atoning death of righteous men, and that (especially Isaiah 53) then became the conceptual material for this new insight. It can be derived only from the events by means of which the primitive Christian texts themselves answer the question concerning the origin and legitimation of their new insight, from the appearances of the risen Jesus and the outpouring of the Holy Spirit (i.e., from the manifestation of the divine installation of the slain Jesus as the prince of life for all men and for all times), and from a divinely given new and life-giving power of understanding. In the face of all questions seeking a better, more rational proof of its truth, the new insight is defenseless; those who represent it can only hope that those who hear it will have their eyes opened to the reality of Jesus in the same way as were their own.

What is the meaning of this phrase "for us"? Theology in the course of centuries has thought out various theories to interpret it, because the primitive Christian texts largely restricted themselves to this assertion "for us" (as, for example, in the words of institution of the Lord's Supper) and because, where they offer more, especially in the writings of Paul, their interpretation cannot be developed into a theory that answers all questions. The theological theories—for example, the satisfaction theory of Anselm of Canterbury, the depiction of the conflict of redemption in Athanasius, the justification Christology of Luther, and Karl Barth's theory of atonement—are theories to help make the meaning of the phrase "for us" more understandable; we are not meant to have faith in them, but are meant to let them help us appropriate the words "for us" in an understanding of faith.

The phrase in any case means that this one stands security for us all. He wills this, and has the power to do it, to stand security for another to the bitter end, and with final saving power for him. He wills and can do this for each and all of us, even where we can expect help neither from ourselves nor from any other human being. Such a situation is assumed to be that of everyone, and it is described in terms of a sentence of law (condemnation to death), of morals (inexpiable guilt), of struggle (hopeless abandonment to captivity in the hands of powerful opponents), or of fate (desperate bondage under demonic powers).

Thus:

(1) The dying of this one man is promised as decisive help for everyone *in extremis,* in the most utter affliction conceivable.

(2) The possibility that one man's dying can be of decisive help for others lies in the fact that here it is not merely an individual man dying for others, but it is God so identifying himself with this one man that what this man suffers is suffered by God himself; here the Jesus who stands surety for us is the God who stands surety for us, and God—no longer remaining untouched in his exaltation—stands surety for us as a brother for his brothers and sisters, or as a friend for his friend.

(3) It is in the light of the greatness of God's intervention that the greatness of our affliction is measured.

(4) This intervention by God happens definitively. In other words, it happens as an action to which we have nothing more to add, in the objectivity and completeness of an event with a determined *hic et nunc* ("here and now") in earthly history. It is as external to our life as that cross on the hill of execution in the Jerusalem of the time of the Roman Caesars, which stands far remote from our

lives and which can only be known by us as something that has already happened. Paul's challenge, "Be reconciled to God" (II Cor. 5:20) does not at all mean that we are reconciled to God only when we allow ourselves to be reconciled to him (namely, by receiving in faith a divine offer of forgiveness). Rather, it means that because God, identifying himself with Jesus, has "changed places" (the original sense of the Greek word for "reconcile," *katallagein*) with the cosmos (the world of men), for that reason the world of men *is* reconciled to him, and consequently every one of us is reconciled also. We are given the power subjectively to live in the light of this objective change in the situation, by this being brought to our knowledge and at the same time promised to us as something that we can grasp, so that we may draw the consequences of an inwardly and outwardly changed way of life: *extra nos pro nobis* ("outside of us for us"), a reality given to us in order to open up new possibilities of life.

As a finished work ("fact of salvation") this is made known by Christian preaching, but not as a fact like, for example, an earthquake, which we can look up in the records but which is far from our life today. It is, rather, an *act*-ion,* an act which has an agent and which continues to operate as an act/word. When the fact of Jesus' death on the cross is made known as an act of Jesus *and* an act of the God who identifies himself with him, all who come to hear it are placed in a new relation to both these agents, who together encounter them: to Jesus, and to him whom he calls his "Father." This new relation is the new reality of their life, their new situation from

---

*TRANSLATOR'S NOTE: The German here contains an untranslatable pun. The word *Tatsache*, "fact," resembles the word *Tat*, "deed" or "action," and Gollwitzer underlines the first syllable to emphasize that this fact is also an action, a sense that has been lost in the modern sense of *Tatsache*.

which their new life possibilities originate.

That primitive Christianity gave expression to this extraordinary view of this particular death is, as we said, not derivable either from historical religious traditions or from psychological causes (e.g., a swing from the depression of the disciples over to the "nevertheless" of faith, and a conquest of the disappointment caused by Jesus' failure to return in the near future, as they had expected). The fact of this new insight is as extraordinary as its content, and that the first witnesses were aware of this is shown by the way that they trace back their insight to nothing other than revelation, to the appearances of the risen Lord and to the Holy Spirit, who disclosed to the witnesses of this act the content, the true significance of the fact of Jesus' death as an act of Jesus and his Father "for us." On the Spirit depends also the fact that we, the hearers and receivers of this revelation, have our eyes opened to the meaning of this "good news" concerning this terrible death. Thus the understanding of this news and the life which flows from it are always just as extraordinary as the news itself.

In trying to achieve theological understanding, it is decisively important not to seek to appropriate the meaning of the New Testament statements about the "exchange" of the world with God through "God in Christ," which takes place in the cross of Jesus (II Cor. 5:19–21), in such a manner that the question is made more easily intelligible and acceptable to us. What is here being said far transcends the capacities of our understanding and consequently remains ever before us as a task for thought. The phrase "for us" always contains much more significance than we have already apprehended.

c. God's identification, in Jesus, with his people and with humanity takes place with all the consequences for us.

(1) *For Israel,* first of all. If this identification means inseparability, then Israel is now the people that can never again be separated from its God—not separated even by its disloyalty and guilt.

(2) At the same time, for those Jews who follow Jesus, the story of Jesus is the authentic interpretation of the Torah given to Israel. For these Jews the Torah reveals itself as essentially the command to live in harmony with this God, i.e., in unquenchable hope for Israel and the whole of mankind, and also in an unconditional self-forgetting love, and to do this in faith, i.e., in trust in the presence and power of this God, who so consistently identifies himself with man, and makes their cause his cause, cost what it may. Faith, hope, and love (I Cor. 13:13) are the central words for the practical consequences, *besides* which there can be no other values, motives, or goals of equal standing, in the light of this central event. They become, therefore, criteria for judging all types of behavior.

(3) Final confirmation is now given to the universal goal of the God of Israel, the *malkuth Adonai,* the Kingdom of God. Through this event this promise is declared by him who gave it as no longer revocable, while he himself has made it for himself no longer revocable. If the earthly Jesus had proclaimed this kingdom as imminent, his hearers do not see this proclamation as contradicted by the death of Jesus and the unchanged state of the world. On the contrary, Easter makes it possible for them to acknowledge the death of Jesus, both as conclusively confirming the promise concerning the Kingdom, and also as teaching that the consummation of the Kingdom will not overtake them like a sudden world catastrophe which makes a sudden end of suffering and guilt. No, Easter teaches rather that the consummation of the Kingdom comes on a *journey* that leads God into suffering, and causes him to go

through further suffering, a journey, however, that has
the promise of fulfillment and the achievement of his
goal.

The expression "Kingdom of God" has the following
meaning in both parts of the Bible:

(*a*) It means not so much an individual event as one
belonging to humanity, a new individual life in harmony
with God, a "blessed" life no longer threatened by guilt
and death, within the context of a similar life of humanity.

(*b*) It means not a fulfillment in the beyond which
would reject the life of this world as irrelevant or hopelessly corrupted. Both the prophetic hope of the Old
Testament and primitive Christianity's expectation of a
second coming relate the hope of the Kingdom of God to
a renewal of this earthly life. However hard this may
seem for us today to imagine, it should have reminded
Christians that the "sanctification of the earth" belongs
no less to the Christian than to the Jewish hope.

(*c*) It means not removal to a situation with happy
conditions of life (comparable to a fools' paradise), so
much as—like the third petition of the Lord's Prayer—
the accomplishment of the divine will in the will of his
creatures, the conformity of the human will with the
divine will, and that on a worldwide scale. The Kingdom
of God is thus identical with a human way of life, both
individual and social. So the promise of the Kingdom of
God looks for a wholly new human society opposed to
the corrupt old society, with a new social way of living. It
is lived in anticipation in new cells of the brotherhood, in
which there is no longer injustice between masters and
slaves, cultivated men and barbarians, citizens and immi-
grant workers, men and women (Gal. 3:28; Col. 3:11),
and these cells are not to be thought of in monastic terms
as isolated islands, but as outward-working, radiating
"cancer cells," which disintegrate the old society, replac-
ing it with new forms of life. If the cancer simile seems

inappropriate, let us take the New Testament picture of the new community as salt, light, and leaven (Matt. 5:13–16; 13:33).

If we are to understand the central position of Jesus in Christian faith, it is all-important that the Jesus event be understood as an act/word: as an event that is not only a historical event but an act of God in space and time. It is not merely a dumb act, but is at the same time a speaking word. Nor is it only a word to be proclaimed and proclaimed again in a prophetic manner, but a word as act, as a fundamental and transforming act; as the achievement of the promised restoration of humanity by the God of Israel. This restoration is accomplished in an act which is preceded by a way—the way of this God with Israel—and from which a way proceeds: the way of the new manner of life which is the result of this act, and is the anticipation of its ultimate accomplishment, its accomplishment in the final reality of the Kingdom of God, when no contradiction or opposition to it will exist anymore, when "every rule and every authority and power" that boasts itself as independent will be destroyed, when he has "put all his enemies under his feet," including "the last enemy," death (I Cor. 15:24ff.).

In the "as yet unredeemed world" (Barmen Declaration, Thesis 5), this world-transforming act of atonement has *already* happened, and has thereby ensured that the way of humanity moves toward its redemption, its liberation, its life. That is the extraordinary hope based on the extraordinary view of the death and the resurrection of Jesus Christ, with which the Christian message confronts every pessimism of destruction which world conditions today place in our way.

RECOMMENDED READING

Flusser, David. *Jesus*. Rowohlts Bild-Monographien, No. 140. 1968.

Kierkegaard, Søren. *Einübung im Christentum. Werkausgabe,* Section 26. Translated by E. Hirsch. 1951. (E.T. *Training in Christianity.* 1944.)

Klappert, Bertold. *Die Auferweckung des Gekreuzigten. Der Ansatz der Christologie Karl Barths im Zusammenhang der Christologie der Gegenwart.* 1971.

Schweizer, Eduard. *Jesus Christus im vielfältigen Zeugnis des Neuen Testaments.* Siebenstern / Gütersloher Taschenbücher, No. 126. 1968.

V

God

The word "God" is in very common use. The God to whom the Bible gives this title is distinguished from the gods of the religions and the God of metaphysics. However, biblical language about God will be found in close connection with these two other uses of the word. The distinction must be drawn so as to prevent confusion and make two things clear: the God of the Bible grants men communion with himself, and this God can make use of men.

We have used the word "God" several times, usually with the further specification "the God of Israel." Thereby the word "God" was brought into connection with a particular people. The second further specification was that, before we spoke of God, we spoke about an earthly man, Jesus of Nazareth, and brought this into a special relation with the word "God." This is remarkable, because everybody is always talking about God. Talk about God is thus no special prerogative of the Jewish-Christian tradition. In all the religions found in history, there is talk of the divine, of God, or of a number of gods. Even Buddhism, without itself leading to faith in God, contains doctrinal statements about gods and the divine. Because we meet this in all religions, religion is commonly identified with teaching about God. The criticism of religion, even Marxist criticism, is wont to concern itself principally with such teaching about God.

It is true that the phenomenon of religion cannot be defined solely in these terms. But because talk of God is universal, it is important that we draw particular attention to the special character of biblical talk about God—both Jewish and Christian. This will decide also in what sense we can speak of religion in biblical faith, and in what sense not. We will not now embark upon the task of searching for a general concept of religion, a project that is repeatedly undertaken and that repeatedly miscarries. There is clearly no universal concept of religion which would cover all phenomena that are in any respect to be regarded as religious. It is precisely the vague and debatable character of the modern concepts "religion" and "religious" that shows that wherever such concepts come to mind, we are dealing with movements of the human spirit and society which go beyond making our daily living, and which seek for a universal interpretation of human life. Such a striving is probably as fundamental and unavoidable as the urge to maintain our physical existence and our life in the face of physical needs. This is the element of truth in Schleiermacher's theory of religion which claims that religious feeling (admittedly too narrow an expression) belongs to the nature of man, and of the old theistic proof *e consensu gentium* (i.e., from the presence of belief in God among all nations). Religion in the sense of such a striving is obviously as old as humanity itself; it cannot be surrendered or extirpated so long as human beings exist. Anyone who dreams of "religion dying out," or even hopes that it will, has not given sufficient thought to this matter, and has also not considered how much that is human would have to die out in order for religion, defined as this striving, to die out also.

Therefore we will not concern ourselves with the concept of religion that is dealt with in the contemporary sociology of religion, nor will we consider the relation between theology and the sociology of religion. We will confine ourselves to the question, How do men, in addition to speaking about man and the world, come to speak about "God"—in some sense or other—and what do they mean when they do so? This time, too, let us build up an approach to the question from outside, and then ask what is the peculiarity of biblical talk about God.

A widely prevalent answer to these questions runs as follows: God is an auxiliary concept and an auxiliary idea of the still unsecularized consciousness of earlier times, used to interpret the world. It is used to articulate every urgent and mysterious reality—reality as it is experienced in the processes of nature, both the regular and the extraordinary processes, and also psychical reality (e.g., ecstatic experiences, charismatic phenomena), the overwhelming character of events and realities in human life which man experiences as blessing him or terrifying him, realities not created by him but coming upon him. To all this he gives the predicate of the divine, i.e., of the superhuman which is stronger than he is, which he cannot dominate, but which dominates him. The words *el* in Hebrew, *theos* in Greek, and *deus* in Latin (to cite only the languages that are important and fundamental for our culture), mean, in the first place, not a name, but a predicate which can describe all manner of things, superhuman powers as they can be experienced in ecstasy, powers external to mankind (powers of nature), and powers more than individual (social powers); the predicate expresses their dominating might, and declares them to be sacred.

The wide-ranging applicability of this predicate is in itself an indication that, when under the influence of the modern consciousness we refrain from the use of such predications, the realities themselves to which the predicate "divine" was formerly ascribed have by no means necessarily disappeared. The gods have not passed away because we no longer call them gods, and the fact that we no longer believe in gods does not mean that we are free of those powers which we earlier called gods. Nor does it mean that there are not plenty of powers in our world today which we treat as gods. The ancient saying "The world is full of gods" is true even today, and has not been refuted by atheism and the abandonment of the use of the predicate of the divine.

That man in the modern age is just as dependent on gods, and relates himself to the gods, is evident when we reflect on the general way in which Luther defines the word "god."

> A god is that power to which a man must look for all good, and in which he must take refuge in all distresses; consequently, to have a god is nothing less than trusting and believing in him heartily; as I have often said, . . . only trust and faith of the heart makes both, god and idol. . . . That on which you set your heart and on which you rely is truly your god.[35]

We shall have to add: What you fear most, and what you see threatening and endangering your life most, that is also your god. For what disposes of us can dispose of us for life or for death. If the striving to achieve a general interpretation of life, of which we were speaking, is a search for meaning, then we can also say: That wherein you think to find the meaning of your life is your god, and that which you fear may cast you into utter meaninglessness is also your god.

In this passage Luther's definition of the word "god" has an intention that is thoroughly critical of religion: trust and fear belong to human existence, which, whatever we might wish, is not wholly under our control, an existence in which we need to receive favor—from whatever source it may come—and which we see daily exposed to all kinds of fatal threats which we fear. The intention of Luther's definition is to lead us to ask whether the powers in which we trust are really worthy of unlimited confidence, and if the powers that we fear are really those from which comes the deepest threat to our lives. This is the purpose of his distinction between God and idol: Who really merits the predicate "God"? And to whom do we relate ourselves absolutely as to God, although he is really only an idol, a false God, an image?

This question converges to some extent with the Marxist criticism of religion, the aim of which is to make clear to people that what they honor, fear, and hold sacred as a divine power that dominates them—namely, authorities, traditions, social structures, and powers of nature—does not really deserve the name of God; that these powers should, rather, be divested of their divine reputation—in order that, as in Hans Christian Andersen's tale about the Emperor's new clothes, we may see them in their secularity, stripped of their divinity, and that we should thus no longer behave as their slaves, but encounter them as free men.

The religious criticism of the Old Testament prophets spoke in like manner of the gods honored by the peoples, the *elim*, whom they scornfully called *elilim*, "little gods," and "nothings," and pointed out that they were "made by the hands of men" and thus were products of human society and projections of the human spirit. This desacralization, as in the other case, is meant to set men free from false respect, enabling them to be fearless in relation to these powers and to hold up their heads and confront them as free men.

The difference, however, between these two forms of religious critique is that the Marxist critique, being modern, springs out of a thoroughgoing rationalism and immanentism, and so makes man depend wholly upon himself, and indeed upon his intelligence and knowledge of dominion. Consequently it operates with a defective doctrine of man, and contests the validity of experiences that are not subject to rational explanation. The prophetic critique, on the other hand, by no means denies the reality of such experiences of superior power, and of that which may stand behind them. We find too in the prophets the rational denial of the existence of the gods, but the emphasis is not laid upon this. The difference—whether the existence of gods, demons, or witches is affirmed or denied on philosophical grounds—is not so great as we are accustomed to think, for if these powers do not exist, there do exist plenty of others which hold us in their powerful clutches, to whom we submit, half in trust, half in fear, sometimes the one, sometimes the other. But for our practical life the difference is all-important that the prophetic critique does not make man depend upon himself and his reason, like the modern forms of the critique of religion. Its aim is, rather, to set him free, to make him autonomous and fearless, by assuring him of the help of another Power—that Power to which in reality he owes his existence, and which is superior to those powers, and thus able to deal with them, so that, from this standpoint, man can venture not to respect these powers and to follow his reason set free from superstition.

The basis of human freedom and fearlessness lies in the unshakable promise of such help; and not in our so easily shaken confidence in our own strength, whether it be the strength of our reason or our other powers.

There is a second way in which men come to speak of God. That is the philosophical and metaphysical way: the language about God focuses itself on the inquiry into the ultimate ground of all being. Here Asiatic metaphysics and Greek metaphysics run parallel, though in the two cases the outlook on life is widely divergent. Here the method is one that transcends individual existence, and consequently also the divine powers of which we spoke, by means of progressively more radical questioning, and, in contrast with the anthropomorphism of the traditional religions, the inquiry is made for that which gives reality to the real, and unity to the manifold, and also (here the inquiry becomes practical and ethical) for what gives meaning to our endeavors: "God" here means the reality which establishes and determines all things, both on this side of the individual existent and beyond it. To describe this reality, the word in current use for "God" is adopted from traditional religion, but now in its significance as that which transcends everything human, radicalized as a limiting concept to a significance transcending all individual existence. The predicate "God," hitherto applicable in the plural, becomes a singular, which is reserved for the ultimate ground of being, in which we, like all individual existents, participate, but to which we can only draw near in an inquiry that continually transcends every foreground—i.e., only in thought, not in experience. What we intend with this radical questioning can never positively be experienced, grasped, and named by us. The true language about it, as Xenophanes of Colophon[36] basically saw, is not the anthropomorphic, but the negative, which describes no properties; or the positive language of superlatives, which precisely in its use of superlatives is only a repetition and modification of the negative. "God" here means the first and last, the only unchangeable reality, the origin of all being and all decay, the origin of our own questionableness and our own questioning.[37]

Of this one God—according to the critical conclusion of ancient philosophical monotheism—there is no revelation; this reality does not speak, and it cannot be spoken to. Powers that can speak and hear, that change and change themselves, do not deserve to be described by the title "God," which has now been thus radically conceived. As limiting concept of our thought and inquiry, God in this sense is the inaccessible mysterious ground of all penultimate and individual existences. One can equally well say, however, that all penultimate and

88 An Introduction to Protestant Theology

individual existences are his revelation, for everything is the foreground to this background—everything, the good and the bad, life and death. This final reality is the ground and abyss of all penultimate reality.

The biblical way of speaking about God stands in a peculiar mediating position between these two other ways of speaking. It is not the result of ever-deepening transcendent reflection, like the second, but, like the first, results from the thrust of concrete reality here in the foreground of our concrete existence. To that extent it *appears* to be a special case of the manner of speech of the traditional religions, arising from religious experiences corresponding to theirs, but, like them, capable of being surpassed by the power of radically transcendent thinking, and, by its advancing rationalization, which unmasks all the foreground gods as false gods, and not the final, all-determining reality. For the biblical God acts and speaks like a power that appears in our midst in the foreground of the world of individual existences, in the same manner as in the traditional religions all the powers which are there called "divine" are asserted to do.

On the other hand, however, this power, this God of biblical faith, is as far superior to the other gods, as critical of them, as little an individual instance of a plurality of gods, and as absolutely singular, as is the God of metaphysics. The God of whom the Bible speaks cannot be transcended by any other, he is *id quo majus cogitari nequit*, a being "than whom nothing greater can be conceived" (Anselm of Canterbury).[38] Over his head no appeal to any higher authority can be made. No deeper truth beyond him can be sought for; what he says, promises, or commands cannot be thwarted or refuted by other words, truths, and events. "Thy word is truth" (John 17:19).

But just this phrase, "Thy word," distinguishes the God of whom the Bible speaks from the two other powers

that have the title of "God" applied to them—the plurality of life-determining and life-endangering powers of the
religions, and the final reality beyond experience, the
God of metaphysics. Neither of these powers has any
word for us—certainly not the background God of metaphysics, for the concept of him excludes it. He cannot
speak, and he cannot be spoken to: that would not be
theoprepes, not "fitting for God," as Xenophanes said,
thereby setting up a metaphysical criterion for that being
which deserves the title of "God." For speaking and
being spoken to would, he said, be occurrences in time,
incompatible with God's timeless changelessness. He is
the silent background and origin of all events, which
cannot be reached or touched by our voices.

The foreground gods can indeed—as is claimed in the
myths—appear, speak, and act, but they do this only from
time to time, according to their mood, and, as soon as the
stories about this are reduced to their essentials, they
show themselves capable of interpretation as stories
about the powers of our existence which in reality
dumbly rule in our life and over it. It goes to confirm our
case that, apart from a few newly discovered Ugaritic
texts, the coming of the majestically uttered word of
YHWH to a prophet in the Hebrew Bible is something
unique in the history of religion. In general, the same
thing is true of the gods as of the God of metaphysics:
"The gods are silent."[39] *Dii homines non curant* ("The
gods do not concern themselves about men"), said Democritus[40] percipiently. To this great, general dumbness
which enfolds human existence, the biblical man of
prayer opposes his confession "Our God comes, he does
not keep silence" (Ps. 50:3).

Thus Martin Buber rightly contrasts the monotheism of
metaphysics with biblical monotheism:

The great deed of Israel is not that it taught of the
one, real, God who is origin and goal of all being, but

that it shows that this God can really be spoken to, can be addressed as Thou; can be confronted face-to-face, can be associated with. True, everywhere that man is found, there prayer is found also, and so it has always probably been. But Israel was the first to understand, and even to experience, life as a being-spoken-to and answering, an addressing and the receiving of an answer. True, the intention of mystery cults in all human societies is to lead into an apparently much more intimate communion with the deity but, as everywhere, where exceptional conditions instead of everyday life are concerned, we can perceive in what is experienced as divine only the man-created picture of a partial appearance of the real God, who is the origin and goal of all being: the little finger of his left hand is called Pan. God in his concreteness as speaker, the creation as language; the Call into nothingness, the answer of things by their coming into existence; the language of creation continues in the life of every creature; the life of every creature as dialogue; the world as word—to proclaim this was Israel's task. It taught, it showed that the real God is the God who can be spoken to, he is the God who speaks.[41]

Apart from the fact that it is surely more correct to speak of this "teaching," this "discovery" of Israel not so much as a deed but as an objective experience, and a task of Israel which resulted from it, Buber here exactly hits on what must be said about the difference between biblical language about God and the two other ways of speaking about God. This includes the language about God in both parts of the Bible, the Old and the New Testament.

The New Testament, under the impression made by the life, death, and resurrection of Jesus, drew further consequences of the "concreteness" of God beyond what it had been possible for the witnesses to God of the Old

Testament to see: a most radical self-identification and act of solidarity of God beyond his communion with Israel and his creation described in the Hebrew Bible, with all the consequences for him and us which have been described in Chapter IV. Because of this identification of God with the creation, in the creature Jesus of Nazareth, Christendom was compelled to speak of God in *trinitarian* terms: of the Creator before and above his creation; of the Creator who, identifying himself with his creation, enters into his creation; and also of the Creator of new knowledge and new life for people of the old life. Christian theology has traced back these three ways of encounter of God with his creatures to the life of the eternal God himself, in which they are based, and has done so with a twofold purpose:

1. First, it should always be clear that in all these encounters it is one and the same God with whom we have to deal, and not a different God on each occasion— e.g., against the opposition of the creator God to the Redeemer God which was taught by the early Christian Gnostic Marcion, whom the church repudiated (in the middle of the second century A.D.). Thus the doctrine of the Trinity serves precisely to protect the *unity* of God which is so important to the Jewish faith, and not to dissolve this unity in a kind of polytheism (tritheism) as the Jewish critics of the doctrine of the Trinity have always feared.

2. Second, we should be certain that God in his eternity is none other than the one who reveals himself here, that is, the one who loves us and declares himself to be one with us, not another *deus absconditus* ("a hidden God") in the background from whom we might expect other, perhaps worse things than from this *Deus revelatus* ("the God of the revelation"). The God who stands surety for us with all the consequences that follow is the one God; above him and behind him there is no other:

"and there is no other God" (Luther). This is the good, indispensable meaning of the doctrine of the Trinity, by means of which the biblical language about God is expounded and brought to our right understanding.

What the language of the Bible says in relation to human life I shall attempt to summarize in two propositions:

1. God grants men communion with himself.
2. God can make use of men.

These two propositions embrace the content of biblical language about God, and consequently the task of theological thinking about God.

1. In regard to the first proposition, that God grants human beings communion with himself: We conclude from what has been said that a fundamental experience must have happened and must continue to happen, which is not confined to those who have felt it powerfully, but which can and must be passed on as a message to others and, indeed, "to all."[42] From this we can see that the essential in this experience is anything but what Rudolf Otto[43] concluded was the characteristics of religious experience, the feeling of awe before the *mysterium tremendum* (the mystery that makes one tremble) and enchantment by the *mysterium fascinosum* (the mystery that fascinates us); both these experiences are in the true sense incommunicable. What is essential in that fundamental experience is rather a message to all, a word. In this word, what we have to do with, however often it is expressed in words, is not individual revelations of supernatural truths (*veritates revelatae*), but, prior to them, and underlying them, a fundamental revelation, a promise which contains the assurance of communion, and indeed *communion with God*—God here understood in the most strictly singular sense, and as final reality, as *summum ens* and *summum bonum*, as being itself (Paul Tillich),[44] not one great power among others.

This is the meaning of the biblical anthropomorphism, the talk of a "personal God." This may seem "primitive," childishly credulous, mythological and liable to be de-mythologized by reflection and abstraction, but in reality it outstrips most daringly every abstraction by synthesizing elements that oppose each other in metaphysical reflection, the infinite and the finite, the absolute and the relative, being itself and the single existent. Of the absolute is said what may only be said of the relative, and for the relative is made possible what otherwise belongs only to the self-subsistent absolute. God makes himself capable of communion with men, and man worthy of communion with God.

What will result from this real communion between creator and creature, between God and man, which contradicts the ontological definition of the absolute and the relative, is the tense *expectation* with which biblical faith accompanies history. What has hitherto arisen from it is the enthralling story—not only of the Bible, but the enthralling manner in which biblical faith tells the story of humanity up to the present, and in the future. Whether there are events in this history which open up encouraging prospects for the future, that is the question which the telling of the story is meant to elicit from us: Is the history of this communion, for the individual and for humanity, in the last resort a history of salvation or one of damnation?

2. All this could be understood in rather a formal manner, if we did not add the second proposition: God can make use of human beings. The conversation is not mere idle chatter about anything and everything; it has a goal, and its purpose is to unite two wills, two subjects to work together. Thus the first proposition implies a second anthropomorphic statement about God, which is also based on the fundamental experience, the word of God: God is *will*, directed to the human will. And because the

will occupies itself in a communion, the conclusion follows: God is an active will that encounters man in history, by means of which history becomes the history of an endeavor in which the eternal will invites and empowers the final will to cooperate. That means that history becomes teleological, and men are deemed worthy not only of communion but of cooperation in the service of this goal. Therefore all the epiphanies in the Bible are stories of commissioning: the two creation stories (Genesis 1 and 2), the appearance of God in the burning bush (Exodus 3), the covenant at Sinai, the baptism of Jesus, the calling of the disciples, the resurrection appearances, and the appearance of Jesus to Paul on the road to Damascus.

At this point we must once more glance at the metaphysical inquiry: the supreme unconcern of the final ground in relation to all individual existents based upon it—and the indifference of its fundamental enabling act by means of which life and death, positive and negative, good and evil, are made possible—could not satisfy even the philosophers. Therefore the question was repeatedly asked about the way from metaphysics to ethics. Even if the final ground has no will, we still ask whether guidelines (norms) for our behavior can be read off from our reflection upon it. How that has happened offers subsequently a wide scope for ideological criticism, i.e., for the observation of how time-conditioned and interest-conditioned norms have been raised to a so-called eternal status.

But however clearly we see through this pretension, the question remains. It is expressed in two forms: (1) We experience claims from within the world which lay unconditional obligation upon us; this is the phenomenon of conscience. (2) From this standpoint we see our actions as our own, for which we have to answer: from which, then, we cannot dissociate ourselves, to which we are held, according to which we are judged. We are aware of a bond of iron between what we do and what we are, between our life and our right to live. If there are only norms, whether historically conditioned or eternal, if there is only the claim laid upon us, with the unconditional accent of our conscience, then our right to life stands or falls with our actions, and the claim laid upon us by the living will of God, who thinks us men worthy to be his co-workers and calls us such, could only infinitely intensify this claim. That is what Christian theology means by the concept of the *law*—abstracted from the Torah of Israel.

But of course the Bible regards the hearing of the word of God, which invites to communion and summons to cooperation, as including the exact opposite of the law, and in this the living character of this divine will shows itself in contrast with the immutability of the norms, to which corresponds the immutability of the ultimate metaphysical background, and also the immutability of that "brazen bond" between doer and deed, between me and my guilt. This connection is an iron prison that we cannot ourselves break open.

> The sins I committed cannot be erased,
> The clever are valued, the bold are praised;
> Only the heart, the heart in my breast
> Has its own infinite guilt confessed.
> *Frank Wedekind*[45]

The one living God with his free will is thus preeminent over the gods, whose function is precisely to be guarantors and vindicators of the laws that obtain in a society and are established as unbreakable and eternally fixed norms. And he is equally superior to the unchangeable final ground which, because of its immutability, is not free to concern itself about our imprisonment. This preeminence shows itself in the fact that God's word, in addition to allowing us fellowship and considering us worthy to be co-workers, contains a third element which alone and at last makes the message of this word a *good* message, an *euangelion*, and without which it would be a message even more productive of fear than the revelations of the gods and reflection on the ultimate ground. The living character and the preeminence of God's will shows itself in the fact that he can break open the prison, the brazen bond between the doer and his deed, that he can free me from that from which I cannot free myself, that he can liberate my future from my past, and thus open it and make it new. This is the meaning of a biblical word which makes "God" a name that releases jubilation, "forgiveness of sins."

Only when this addition has been made is the message of the word of God completely described. "To the Lord belongs forgiveness" (Dan. 9:9). To forgive is to give away and to put away that which no power in the world can put away. Therefore it is a possibility that belongs to God alone. "Who can forgive sins but God alone?" (Mark 2:7). Who can forgive sins except him who is the source of the unconditional claim, and except him who can do the impossible? Here the responsibility of the doer for his deed is taken with absolute seriousness, which is shown by the fact that here forgiveness is seen as the miracle of all miracles, and as an action that is not cheap, but one that costs him who forgives the pledge of his own life, by taking on himself the death of the sinner. And here this seriousness in its full extent is only experienced through removal by the new fellowship, by the new assurance of communion and cooperation which constitute forgiveness. All this is meant by the words of Paul about the justification of the godless (Rom. 4:17; 5:6).

But at the same time we must also note that it is just in this new guarantee that forgiveness consists. It does not suppress the call to cooperation, it does not constitute its end but its beginning; it gives it a new foundation. The communion between God and man does not have forgiveness as its goal, but the call to cooperation. This is therefore also the goal of forgiveness, the new installation in a working partnership. The Reformers' discovery of forgiveness as the "key" to Holy Scripture had its justification in the face of the fear-awakening preaching of righteousness by works and of judgment in the medieval church, but through its one-sidedness it brought the accompanying danger that, in the exegesis of the Reformers and the pietists, salvation was regarded as completed by the reception of forgiveness. With this limitation to the salvation of the accepted sinner the universal world-embracing tendency of God's communion with men was lost to sight, as was the call of man to work with God in his purpose, in the *Kingdom of God*. Therefore today we can only speak truly of forgiveness and justification as the liberating act of God, which stands in the context of God's great historical enterprise, in the context of the history of the Kingdom of God, and in the context of God's Kingdom as a history.

RECOMMENDED READING

Buber, Martin. *Gottesfinsternis. Betrachtungen zur Beziehung zwischen Religion und Philosophie.* 1953. (E.T. *Eclipse of God.* 1953.)

Geyer, Hans Georg. "Atheismus und Christentum." In *Evangelische Theologie,* 30. Jahrgang, 1970, pp. 255–274.

Iwand, Hans Joachim. *Glauben und Wissen.* Nachgelassene Werke, Vol. 1. Munich, 1962.

Jäger, Alfred, *Gott. Nochmals Martin Heidegger.* 1978.

Jüngel, Eberhard. *Gott als Geheimnis der Welt.* 1977.

————. *Gottes Sein ist im Werden.* 3d ed. 1976.

Miskotte, Kornelis Heiko. *Biblisches ABC. Wider das unbiblische Bibellesen.* 1976.

————. *Der Gott Israels und die Theologie.* 1975.

van Peursen, Cornelius A. *Das Wort "Gott." Erwägungen eines Philosophen.* 1969.

VI

The History of the Church as a Question Concerning the Church

The church is the fellowship of those who through the gospel become the subjects of a new life. They are at the same time old and new men. For this reason, as individuals and as a fellowship, they are the battleground for the attack of the new life upon the old life. The history of the church is the history of the victories and the defeats in the struggle between the two ways of life. The Lord of the new life, Jesus Christ, is consolation and hope in the face of all defeats.

Two Subjects, God and Man

Now *we* are the theme—a change from the earlier chapters, in which *we* were the theme only as those addressed by the action of another. It is a decisive characteristic of the biblical message that it is the message about the action of another upon us; it speaks always of *two*, who *never* are fused into one (as mysticism would have it). These two are not fundamentally one, nor will they become identical when the goal is reached. This identity thinking of mysticism (Greek and Asiatic) has always been opposed by the Jewish-Christian tradition through its reference to the strict limitations imposed by our creaturely nature. The longing for identity is understandable as a critical expression of the social experience of division and isolation—both in our relations with others and in our manipulation of nature—as a longing for unity with others and with the whole. But this longing does not know what it lacks; its thought continues exactly along the same road that led it into trouble, the road of the will to independence. Even the universe, even God, in whom it longs to be absorbed, if it should succeed in its absorption, would only be as lonely a monad as the lonely monad that longs for the merging of its solitude, and seeks for it only by being merged in a still greater solitude.

The God of the Bible is not and is never the solitary God, and does not wish to be so. He is not solitary as a monotheistic God who then needs the world to do away with his solitude. God does not need the world, because "already in himself"[46] he is not solitary. Rather, in himself (and this is the meaning of the doctrine of the Trinity) he is loving and loved, "an eternal furnace full of love" (Luther). What he already is in himself, that he is and does also outwardly, in "overflowing" love (Rom. 5:5) toward his creation, which he freely called into being—not out of need and longing. Love is, according to Hegel's definition, identity of the nonidentical—and this is the highest, beyond which there is no higher, not even a more intimate union through mutual absorption. For this supposedly higher state would in reality be less, namely the solitude of the immovable, immutable whole that rests in itself, the absence of life: Nirvana as the final identity of being and nothing. But in biblical thought, being is as opposed to nothing as life is to death, and life is always a social existence, movement between different beings, fellowship between different beings. Love and life are—both etymologically and in fact—the same thing.

And so, therefore, the biblical message is always speech between different beings which are irrevocably different, and that strict boundary between Creator and creature has nothing disappointing in it: it is not the condemnation of man to a final duality, which can be transcended by longing, the urge toward a possible transcendence of this duality in a final unity, or the message concerning it. It is, rather, the ontological ground of the possibility of love, the being of man in the presence of God, different from God, before God, vouchsafed by love, and destined for identity in love, not an identity of being with God. It is a difference whose removal would not be life, but death. What is to be removed is the cause of division in this duality, the opposition of creature and Creator, the sin of man and the anger of God concerning sin—this is to be removed through the togetherness of love, which is the original destiny of the creature.

For this reason, biblical faith does not long with mysticism to be absorbed in God; nor does it long to eliminate the confrontation of God and man, but rather regards that as the temptation of the ancient serpent: *Eritis sicut Deus,* as a mode of the revolt of the creature against the Creator. "If there were a God—how could I tolerate not to be God?" (Nietzsche).

Not only in mysticism but also in the atheism which Karl Barth[47] rightly regarded as akin to mysticism *and* in the modern theology which makes concessions to this atheism (and thus in fact regresses from Judaism to Hellenism), man is thrown back into his solitude. This is true both of the "death of God" theology and of an existentialist theology that ventures to speak no more of the existence of God, nor, consequently, of the confrontation of God and man. There man longs for a fulfillment that is conceived in terms of his solitude, and so is not a fulfillment of love, or only a fulfillment in the love of man for man, and which thus falls once more within the horizon of a humanity solitary in nature and in the universe. Biblical faith reaches beyond the social fellowship of man with man, and sees this as based on the social fellowship between the Creator and his creatures. This fellowship is the most beautiful and highest thing that can come to flower for the creature, a happiness beyond which there could only exist an equality with God (i.e., a final solitude of a totality identical with God, which could only be the final misfortune of solitary existence). For this reason the creature in biblical faith is *glad* to be a creature, and glad to stand under the Creator. This subordination to the Creator is, as we said, the ontological precondition that makes possible a fellowship of love with the Creator.

Expressed in Karl Barth's formula, this means that the creation is the external ground of the covenant, its ontological precondition, just as the covenant is the internal ground of the creation, its meaning and therefore the goal of the divine action in creation, in forgiveness, in the reconciliation through Jesus Christ, in the bringing of the Kingdom of God. The Kingdom of God is, indeed, as Ernst Bloch says, the kingdom of man, and the *homo revelatus* is given at the same time as the *Deus revelatus*. But it is a fellowship of love, neither an absorption of man in God (mysticism) nor an absorption of God in man.[48] The happiness of man is *not* to be as God, but to be his child and covenant partner. "To be lowly in relation to God, that is the glory of the creature."[49]

The Attack of Change

Just because of this confrontation we must always keep both sides in view—certainly remembering the irreversibility of the relation between God and man, but not in such a manner as to speak only of God's being and actions, without man being made the theme of our discussions also. There is a Barthianism that makes things easy for itself, which makes this irreversibility an excuse for speaking "only of God," and of man only in a few comfortable general terms (creature, sinner, justified man). Correspondingly, then, eschatology and the doc-

trine of the church never get beyond treatment in gener-
alities—and the consequence of this is that the contemporary reality of the church is only exposed to criticism
by the message of the Kingdom of God in a harmless and
abstract manner. It is possible to escape from it by
referring either to the difference between the true
church and the empirical church or to the hidden presence of the true church in the empirical church; in both
cases the danger for the empirical church is averted. We
cannot permit ourselves this easy way out. In this confrontation of God and man we are an extremely important
factor, at any rate more important than we would be
outside this confrontation, and so we are forbidden to
take ourselves—i.e., ourselves as we in fact are—anything but seriously. We are those to whom is spoken an
eternal word of affirmation, and, answering to this, on us
is laid an extraordinary claim. Both of these are directed
to this temporal existence of ours, and thus also to our
empirical reality, which even we can experience and
perceive, and indeed they are directed to it as an enterprise whose purpose it is to save it and make it serviceable here on earth.

In what way does this saving enterprise, which is
named Jesus Christ, reach and lay hold of my life today?
Various ways are conceivable:

1. One way is that of historical causality. For example,
at Sempach and in other battles the Swiss secured the
freedom of their children for centuries. What fathers do
has a positive and a negative effect on the lives of their
children and grandchildren. Through the mediation of
Christian preaching Jesus too has certainly produced and
still today produces an astonishing aftereffect. But this
influence of his ideas (or the ideas ascribed to him) is not
nearly identical with that divine saving enterprise, and
still less powerful is the historical influence of the
actions of Jesus, which even at that early date was

minimal. For by his actions he has had no influence upon the path of world history—their influence does not reach us.

2. A second way can be thought of as that of the effect of hidden powers proceeding from Jesus Christ. We moderns have few categories for such things, but they are to be found in the mystery cults and also in the Catholic sacramental doctrine; perhaps they are akin to the concept of mana, which we find in comparative religion: hidden powers permeate humanity like leaven, and one participates in them through ritual methods.

3. A third way is conceived of by the New Testament, and was worked out especially by the Reformation theologians. The enterprise of salvation, which broke into our reality with concentrated force at one point in history, lays hold of the contemporary and later world through the medium of the "message." Through bearers who have themselves been apprehended, a report is mediated to us of the saving event, and in this report the object is at the same time the true subject. That is to say, the report about the Savior is the means whereby the Savior, from his unique place in history, lays hold on me and breaks into my life to save and to transform. Not the report as such, not the mediating power of the intermediary, but the Savior himself with *his* power, with his "Spirit," takes the message and the mediatory activity of the messenger as an instrument for his entry from there to here.

In any case, we are concerned with change—and indeed with thoroughgoing, total change; no reforming, but revolutionary change of this everyday human reality of the cosmos (John), and both individual and social change, change of *my* reality and of the reality of *society*. Its *status quo* calls for the divine enterprise of salvation, makes it necessary, and necessary not as a reform but as a revolution, i.e., radically and totally necessary; its *status quo* is here attacked; both I and the whole of society must come out of this attack radically changed.

But if the attack is made neither through the medium of historical causality nor through magical transformation, but through the transmission of a message, then we must inquire more precisely for the media of this message. A message can be passed on in different ways: *(a)* as mere information (neutrally, by satellite); *(b)* by means of committed witness. The effect of the message thus mediated is the rise of a new society through the conjunction of persons who have experienced revolutionary renewal. *The new group,* as a human group which is always at the same time interpreting its life, is, as a first result, also the medium of the saving assault upon the *status quo.*

Then it is clear that the transmission of the message as the means of the saving attack is effected in a very *human* way, by the telling of a story, by argument, by conversation, by example, by the transforming influence of a changed life upon its environment, not in the inhuman way of magic, nor by word of command armed with the sanction of threats. But this *human* way is also the *problem;* first it must be illustrated by considering my case as an individual.

I am not deprived of the freedom of taking up my own position, as I would be by magic and the word of command. Let us take for granted that the message encountered me in the most authentic manner—it does not change me and my behavior (as magic and the word of command would do) at a blow. Its attack meets my resistance. I become a battlefield. If my resistance does not succeed in excluding it, the message makes repeated successful counterattacks. The result is alternating defeats and victories, and my life will consist of sometimes very stable, sometimes very changing combinations of contrasted and conflicting life-styles: those of the new life and the old. If I can no longer exclude the too-sharp onset of the new life, I shall attempt to set limits to it, at

least to exclude it from parts of my life in which the
change threatens to remove the ground of my existence,
without which I believe that I could not live. Or I shall
try to preserve ways of behavior and thinking on which
my heart is especially set. I shall then try to resolve the
dilemma of the rich young ruler (Mark 10:17–22) in such
a manner that I can "both have my cake *and* eat it," have
my riches *and* my discipleship of Jesus. I shall try to
serve both masters and, by means of some kind of two-
kingdom theory, to change the struggle that so oppresses,
nay, tears me asunder, into as stable a compromise as
possible, into an armistice "with my head a heathen and
my heart a Christian" (F. H. Jacobi); justified in faith, in
life a sinner (cf. Rom. 6:1); in private life living according
to the Sermon on the Mount, as a member of society
living according to its laws (thus the schematism of a
degenerate but traditional Lutheran two-kingdom theory).

The aim is always to save the supposed necessities and
indispensabilities of my life from the attack of the message, to weaken the revolutionary gospel to a partial
reform and repair of my life that, in other respects,
continues to run along the old lines—both in practice and
theory. In such an activity the formation of attenuating
theories, and a theology justifying this compromise,
plays an important part; its aim is to give stability to the
compromise and avert the challenge of the attack of the
message, indeed to give the transmission of the message
to me and to others a form that allows the message itself
to have only a partial reforming influence. The question
of whether theology, my private theology, just as much as
the public theology of the church, serves the radical and
total character of the attack of the gospel on the reality of
the *status quo* or instead blunts it, domesticates it, and
renders it harmless—that is the criterion of all Christian
theology.

If it does the former, then it contributes at least to

keeping the struggle going, and that is, even when the message is repeatedly defeated in my life, better than the standstill of compromise which—even if its intention is to guarantee and stabilize the partial victory of the gospel—signifies only a permanent defeat of the gospel.

The Church as Battlefield Between the New Life and the Old

What we regard as the necessities of life are always social realities, for without them, and outside of society, no human life can be accomplished. In addition to the defense of private predilections from the attack of the new life, what is at stake is the defense of these supposed necessities of life, and this shows itself particularly when we pass from the battlefield of the individual life to the new group constituted by the conjunction of individual lives, which as such represents a society within society. If it is possible for the individual largely to isolate himself as a hermit from society, this is much less possible for the group; and neither of them can do it at all, if it belongs essentially to their new existence that both through their existence and their action they should mediate the attack of the message on the whole of society. Emigration out of society, retreat to an island, would then be only another form of the limitation of the message to one partial sphere of life, namely to the Christian sphere, and a denial of the totality of the divine attack of salvation which aims at the totality of life, and consequently at the totality of society, and the totality of our relations to the society that surrounds us.

If we individuals are transformed into a battlefield by the attack of the message, that is inevitably true of the new group—the church. It too will never represent—any more than we individuals do—the victory of the gospel in visible holiness, but the fluctuating conflict of the gospel. Its holiness, i.e., its newness, will be a hidden quality, just like the holiness of us individuals. Not absolutely hidden, because the new life is already present and effects visible changes. But it will be relatively hidden, because the new life from time to time breaks through, and is beaten back, and breaks through in a fluctuating campaign of battle. Just as individuals are at the same time *justi et peccatores* ("righteous persons and sinners"), so the church is at the same time *sancta ecclesia* and *ecclesia peccatrix* ("a sinful church"). Here too the formation of theological theory will have an important function; will it advocate the radical and total character of the evangelical attack, or will it advocate its limitation?

Corresponding to the social character of the church, its own structuring as a group will be of special importance for its influence outward on the surrounding society, for its availability as a medium for the attack of the gospel on society. At the same time, as a group the church will be subject to special pressures from the surrounding society, and either it will transmit the pressure, with its temptations, to the individual members in its midst, or it will defend them against it and strengthen them in their opposition to it. This is what makes the third thesis of the Barmen Declaration so important, because in it the significance of the church is seen not only in the proclamation of the word—as is traditional in Lutheranism—but also in its "order," which we are to think of as including both the forms of its organization and all the forms of its life as a fellowship.

Mission as Dependent on Its Origin

What we have said above describes in an abstract way the fundamental problems of the whole of church history, and we must now discuss this in more detail in the light of what we have said. As we do so, our starting point with the individual Christian as a battlefield should keep us constantly mindful that what happens in the church only repeats what constantly happens in individual life. This will keep us from making facile criticism against the church. Here there is a continuous process of reciprocal reflection: the course of the individual life is reflected in the life of the church, and the contemporary condition of the church is reflected in the life of the individual. Thus neither side can excuse itself and blame the other, for the church should be a good example to us individuals, and I, the individual, should represent the best of the church, in order to draw the others after me.

What holds good for the individual holds good for the church; I am identical with my history, but I am constantly called (by the gospel!) to transcend my history. So the church is identical with this history of two thousand years, but is always called to transcend its history. For it is not an end in itself, not already in itself fulfillment; nor is it a religion or world outlook, which only interprets what is before it and helps us to live in it and to find meaning in it; it lives in the not-yet, eagerly pressing forward, and its goal of service is to be the transmitter of the message, the instrument of the divine saving enterprise. That it is not there for itself but for this service, this is the criterion of its life. And it is part of its singularity that this criterion which points its way forward comes to it from its origin, chronologically from behind, out of the past. This is connected with the fact that its incompleteness comes from a completed work, its service for the future of the Kingdom of God arises from the promise contained in the bridgehead of this Kingdom in earthly realities created by the historical Jesus Christ. Because this history reaches out to us in all later ages through the medium of the message, the primordial form of the message is also its authentic, canonical form. The church came into being through the primordial form of the message ("apostles and prophets," Eph. 2:20); and by assimilating itself in thought, speech, and action to its origin, which was mediated through the primordial form of the message, can it preserve its identity and recover it (we leave out of consideration all necessary interpretative processes for the transmission of the gospel *today*).

Therein lies the incomparable significance of Holy Scripture for the church. The church was of one mind on this point since the formation of the canon; but men did not begin to draw decisive consequences from this until the Reformation. The authority of the Bible was no new invention of Luther; it was always acknowledged. Luther's significance consists in the proclamation of the principle *sola scriptura,* Scripture as *unica norma et judex* ("unique norm and judge") of the church (Formula of Concord; cf. Chapter III, above).

What that signifies for the history of the church the "old believers" of the sixteenth century perhaps guessed better than the Reformers themselves, in their opposition to it and in their claim that the church tradition should have equal authority *alongside* Scripture. For *sola scriptura* means that the origin which makes itself known as authentic in the beginning judges over the future development. As the coming one is identical with him who came, and no other calls us forward than he who two thousand years ago was among us, so there calls us forward the voice of the origin, with which it began, the witness to the origin in the beginning. By acknowledging the Bible, the church in every possible time, and throughout the whole course of history, submits itself to the critique of its origin.

The Source as Critique of the Stream

How will it stand up to this critique? "Most sources are not in agreement with the course of the river" (Jean Cocteau). They cannot determine it beforehand, they cannot govern it, it is governed rather by the late condi-

tions to which the streams are exposed. The impotence of
the source in relation to these later conditions is taught
by the whole of history, and in particular by church
history. Very soon, indeed, in the further course of the
river the source is hardly any longer recognizable; it
owes both its historical greatness and its course less to its
source than to other tributaries that enter it—and one
would also have to speak of the pollution by sewage
which today is so urgent a problem! How much of the
source water of the Danube is still present at Ulm, at
Passau, at Budapest—or even at Immendingen, after a
great proportion of the original water has seeped away
and flowed into Lake Constance!

The medieval feudal church, the church of the Cru-
sades, of the Inquisition, of the witch burnings, of white
colonialism; the throne-and-altar church of the Lutheran
authoritarian state; the church of the war sermons of
1914–1918, of the archbishops of Saigon and Palermo, of
the Portuguese church in Mozambique, the South African apartheid church and, yes, of Bishop Hanns Lilje's
beating the drum for the retiring Defense Minister F. J.
Strauss in 1965; the church of Cardinal Döpfner which
identified itself with entrepreneur capitalism, the deco-
ration and ritual of an episcopal conference, but also of a
worthy conference of Protestant pastors, of Billy Gra-
ham's evangelistic mission "Korea for Christ," with its
homage paid to the Dictator Park, and under the protection of his army and police; and lastly of the prayer of the
American army chaplain for the Christian bomb on
Hiroshima in 1945—what does the source have to do
with this course of the Christian stream, although this
whole stream unceasingly appeals to it and claims to
submit itself to its criticism? If there is a proof of
historical materialism and its thesis of the impotence of
ideas, it is church history. "The idea has always exposed
itself to ridicule, where it was not conjoined with inter-

est," write Marx and Engels in *The German Ideology*. New class interests, direct material interests, and interests expressed in terms of spiritual and psychological need ever mingle with the Christian message. When the interest of the ruling class of a whole world empire allies itself with the message, it becomes a world religion and takes over the political and social task of earlier national religion, the inner stabilization of the existing system of exploitation and domination, and the whole further course of the stream up to the present day is unthinkable without this alliance of the church and social power; we are all its heirs and, in spite of all changes, we are still right in the middle of it.

Let us remain a little longer with the parable of the source and the stream. The water of the source is still contained in the stream, even if sometimes in extreme dilution. Still in the Masses and Services of the Crusaders, Grand Inquisitors, and glorifiers of war, the origin is present in the Bible readings; it is heard, certainly profoundly misunderstood, but no earthly calculator and no historical observer can count where and how often it has been heard with effect. Precisely this is part of the hidden reality of the Kingdom of God, which is still a reality, i.e., an effectual power. We have it to thank that the water from the source, in spite of all admixture and all dilution, has come down to us, and penetrates even into our life. That is the consolation when we contemplate church history, this "hodge-podge of error and violence"(Goethe). It is a consolation not to be underestimated, because, like every biblical consolation, it is one that places us under immediate obligation If the water of the source has reached us, then it lays claim on us—just as if we were contemporaries (Kierkegaard) with the first witnesses at the very beginning—in order to receive and to realize, in action and in life, the tasks to which the source summons us, and neither the course of the stream hitherto nor the admixture and the dilution can serve us as an excuse not to follow the challenge.

The dilution we have mentioned has admittedly a very grave consequence: the water from the source reaches us—we can have no pious illusions about that!—as a part of the stream within the limits of its present place, limits set by the given circumstances. How much of it we hear and obey is in the first place determined by these boundaries. Limited by the alliance of the church with the dominant social powers, the transmission of the message was so controlled that the source water could have no decisive influence upon the course of the stream, or even allow the stream to overflow the limiting banks; i.e., in the preaching of the church, the message was so transmitted that it could not call into question that alliance and the accompanying social structures.

These structures, however, are determined by two fundamental convictions: (1) The riches of the earth are not enough for all to have an equal share. (2) Therefore the good life is possible only at the expense of others. On these convictions rest the class structure of society, the system of domination which secures it, and the struggle to appropriate the world's wealth that continues to this day.

That the message of the Kingdom of God is antithetical to this is at once clear. In that message the invitation to faith and the invitation to love belong together inseparably. As an invitation to *faith* it says: God, the Creator, cares for you and for all; there is enough for all. As an invitation to *love* it says: You must not, and you do not need to, live at the cost of others! This is not the good life; the good life is the life for others. Let them live at your cost as God in Christ lets us live at his cost!

Not limited to special areas, but valid for the totality of life, the message exposes the way of life according to these two fundamental principles as a false, death-bringing life of enmity to God, and invites us to break with it and to begin instead a new life in contradiction with it. For the existing social systems, however, such disclosure and such invitation is not at all to be desired, so they must take care that this opposing conception of life is kept within "reasonable bounds," by keeping the groups concerned small, marginal bohemian groups, hippies, ashrams, which can even be useful as a safety valve of the acquisitive society. But if through special circumstances the group has greatly expanded, then that which is dangerous in its life, or at least in its view of life, is socially dangerous and must be neutralized, and that can be done in several ways. One way of neutralizing this opposing conception of life is the removal of the hope of the Kingdom of God to an absolute distance from the earth and the present, so that the latter remains untouched and the hope remains a mere consolation which makes no demand. Another way is the displacement of faith to one side of active life, i.e., to the inwardness of feeling or to the official sphere of formal affirmation of dogma. Still another way is the individualization of preaching with consequent limitation of life-changing to the private circle. A fourth way is prevention of the formation of communities of the new life with an effect that irradiates society; instead of this, such fellowships are reduced to controllable groups within equally well controlled church organizations. These are the main characteristics of the methods by which the gospel and the church are accommodated to the class society and made harmless, indeed made useful for the function of a religion of stabilization.

This does not mean that we should think that this is a work planned by some General Staff of the ruling classes. The process has rather happened "naturally," as Marx would say. It is not "the church" that has accommodated itself, so that we could blame it today for this reason.

"The church" is indeed an abstraction. The church consists at any time of concrete human beings who bring their own interests of the day, their needs, longings, and passions into the church. And not only do they bring their individual interests, about whose correction vigilant church preaching has always concerned itself, but equally (and still more deep-seated, because hardly conscious) those collective interests which have become "objective spirit" in traditions, in morals, in systems of law, and so forth. Here too, one cannot have one's cake and eat it. If faith is not "the possession of all" (II Thess. 3:2), we still wish to have everyone in the church (through the ordinance of Baptism), in which case everyone and not faith will determine the life of the church. But "everyone" here means the society of the old life, representing itself as a hierarchy of privileges whose standards of value and conviction we have internalized. Its methods of production are deeply stamped upon us, we participate in them daily, and our conversion to the gospel has by no means liberated us from them at a blow. We carry with us its motivations indeed in such a manner that both we and the church become thereby the battleground between the old life and the new. Indeed, that is what happens in the best case! In the people's church indeed, without any questions being asked, the current presuppositions of the existing order—that is, what people take for granted as necessary, indispensable, and inevitable—carry the day without challenge, and ensure that the water of the source should flow only within the confines strictly laid down for it. It is not the distress of one man only, but the distress of nearly two thousand years of church history that is expressed in Johann Sebastian Bach's cantata *Watch and Pray:*

> Even seeking a heavenly goal
> Our body holds captive our soul.

The world with its deceit,
Lays snares for godly feet.
The spirit is willing,
But the flesh is frail:
This forces from us
A sorrowful wail.

With this insurance of society against the attack of the
new life, the transmission of the message is robbed of an
essential dimension; i.e., it becomes *heretical. Hairesis*
(fundamental meaning: "choice") is, according to Karl
Barth,[50] a "capricious selection of individual points from
the whole of the revelation which, since the Christological center is missing, are made 'subsidiary centers' and
place the proclamation of the church in the service of
alien interests." The different large and small groups in
Christendom have zealously hurled the charge of heresy
at one another, and justified their separation by means of
it. But if we take seriously the self-submission of all of
them to the source which is continually present in Holy
Scripture, then we can hardly conceal from ourselves the
fact that the origin condemns them all. There has scarcely been a nonheretical group in all the centuries of
church history, nor is there one today. Even the effort to
obtain a doctrine as true as possible to Scripture—and to
obtain official standing for a confession in closest accord
with Scripture—which marked the churches that
emerged from the Reformation of the sixteenth century,
does not deliver the church concerned from heresy, as is
thought in this tradition. For not only does the attack of
the new life upon the individual old life belong to the
transmission of the message, but so does the attack upon
the old life of the collective, with which the individual
life is closely bound up, the attack upon "public sin"
(Hans Ehrenberg)[51] and upon social conditions in which
the motivations of individuals have taken objective form,
and by which the motivations of individuals in their turn

are determined. And to the transmission of the message belongs not only the witness of the word, of preaching, of doctrine, of confession, but also the new life-style, and that as the life of a fellowship, the new social life of "the community of brothers" (Barmen Declaration, Thesis 3). In it—even if still under the conditions of the old aeon—life is already lived in anticipation in the life-style of the Kingdom of God, and so *metanoia,* repentance, still manifests itself in protest against the oppressive and demanding conditions of the old aeon. This knowledge has repeatedly led to the formation and resistance of smaller groups in opposition to the great churches because, judged by this standard, the heretical character of the great churches could no longer be overlooked. But even these smaller groups had to pay their tribute for their inclusion in the old society. Even their movement of resistance remained partial, and thus became heretical in its turn, and when it was very determined, isolated itself in separate islands.

The Lord of the New Life as the Hope of the New Life
The result seems to give cause for nothing but depression and resignation. Historical materialism seems to be vindicated all along the line. That the water of the source still flows in the stream, even in such dilution, seems a very poor consolation. But precisely at this point we must leave the always inadequate parable; it leads to a naturalistic way of thinking which reckons only with quantitative factors and causalities. Just because of its highly problematical connection with the source, church history confronts us with decisions; it does not allow us merely to look on as spectators, nor to make do with a negative result. Because in it and through it the source is present, however diluted, it confronts us with the question of how much we trust this source; and this is a question we cannot evade by referring to the obvious powerlessness

of the source, as proven by church history. For this is not a disagreeable surprise and disillusionment that contradicts what was said originally. For there we see, not a splendid and powerful figure who then lamentably fails or miscarries, but even there we see the powerlessness that is evident in Him who was cast out by the world that was too strong for Him and hanged on the gallows. Even on Golgotha the powerlessness of the new life in confrontation with the overwhelming power of the old life has been proclaimed, and it is attested by the inscription on the cross.

No one who ventures upon the new life can complain that he has been left in the dark concerning the overwhelming power of the old life in himself and in the society which has left its mark upon him, and for which he bears a share of responsibility. But if, in spite of this, he has ventured upon the new life, he has done so because hope has been awakened in him by the resurrection of Jesus Christ; by the resurrection of the new life, the hope has been kindled that there dwells in the new life a possibility that is not given to the old life, namely the power to reawaken even in the face of deadly refutation, and finally to prevail. The new life has encountered him, not merely as an idea, a longing, a daydream such as Bloch envisaged, but as a subject, a powerful Lord who can cope with the victorious world, and who is powerful precisely in his defeats. He who ventures upon the new life recalls the concrete message about him. It is not the message about an idea, but the message about this subject and his story. And that is a story of death and life, of fatal defeat and life risen out of this defeat. It reminds him that he can exist in the new life only because of the covenant with this subject, and that in his own journey too, the powerlessness of his covenant partner, like his power over death, will be visible.

To sum up: Our own life history, like the history of the church, confronts us with nothing less than the question of *faith.* How much do we trust the subject who has not left us in the dark concerning himself? "Lo, I have told you beforehand" (Matt. 24:25). In spite of the result that we spoke of, this confidence alone enables us without dismay to begin again to take seriously the origin as a contemporary reality, in spite of the discredit thrown upon it by the previous course of the stream, and to take it seriously today as a continuing new possibility for myself.

For this reason church history, like the life story of the individual Christian, over and above that empirical record, is a story of ever-new beginnings. In ever-new beginnings of individuals and groups the origin was and is potent, it bursts present heretical limitations and creates the event of new life, and even if this repeatedly shows limitations because of the individual and social environmental conditions of the old aeon, yet that is every time a sign that confirms faith in the origin. The chain of these signs is the authentic history of the church's faith.

If we take it seriously, and if, because of this, we also take seriously the fact that the origin is a subject, then at last we shall also take seriously the fact that the church is an *event,* and, indeed, an event that we cannot bring about, since it is brought about by the original subject, i.e., the Savior who lays hold of our old life. We cannot of ourselves charm it into existence, cannot realize it by planning and organization; nor can we by these means pass it on, and retain it in life. "The wind blows where it wills" (John 3:8). Our organizing can help the church to become event, not more; i.e., it can contribute to the audibility of the message, so that from time to time, *ubi et quando visum est Deo* ("where and when God pleases," Augsburg Confession, Art. 5), the church becomes event, and, within this event, the life of the fellowship receives an order that corresponds to the new life and expresses it, and not the old life.

The result is that, when we speak of the church, we must not look at our organization, not at *the* history of the church, but at these events, both at the beginning and at repeated intervals in the course of church history. The church organizations, however—which we are accustomed, far too easily, to describe as "The Church"—are at best our attempts to serve the event of "the church," are often enough our attempts to hinder this event, or, at least, so to canalize it that it adapts itself to the stream of the old life in which we are immersed. An essential part of our ever-renewed beginning is the continually renewed attempt to change the organization of the church from a hindrance into a serviceable instrument for the event of "the church," for Him who alone can make us the church.

RECOMMENDED READING

Fischer, Martin. *Überlegungen zu Wort und Weg der Kirche.* 1963.

Houtart, François, and Rousseau, André. *Ist die Kirche eine antirevolutionäre Kraft?* 1973.

Kupisch, Karl. *Kirchengeschichte I–IV.* Urban-Taschenbücher, Nos. 168–171. 1973–1975.

Moltmann, Jürgen. *Kirche in der Kraft des Heiligen Geistes. Ein Beitrag zur messianischen Ekklesiologie.* 1975.

Schellong, Dietrich. *Bürgertum und christliche Religion.* In *Theologische Existenz heute,* No. 187. 1975.

VII   Christianity and Judaism

Judaism and Christianity appear to be two different religions. But if the New Testament is taken seriously, the church and Israel belong together as two communities of God of different kinds bound together by the Jew Jesus of Nazareth. In opposition to the anti-Jewish tradition in the Christian churches, today the recognition of this consanguinity and of its significance is a central theological task.

Anyone who speaks of Christianity must inevitably speak also of Judaism. And inevitably the manner in which one speaks of Judaism, and of the connection between Christianity and Judaism, shows how he understands the Christian message. This holds not only for the sphere of morals—although it must be admitted that the sphere of morals was never something to be taken for granted. The polemical relationship between Christians and Jews grew up very early, found its expression in some violent utterances of the New Testament about the Jews (which had a further unfortunate heritage in the history of the church), and created the first, and for centuries the only, minority problem for the Christianized peoples of Europe, who were able to exercise tolerance of the Jewish minority in their midst or, as more frequently happened, to give full vent to their intolerance of them.

    The fact that, in contrast with other people of different faiths—who were not tolerated—the Jews were allowed to live, and that they were subjected to pogroms, came from the same spirit of insolence and contempt. They were allowed to live as witnesses of the Passion of Jesus

Christ, spared for the curse of God, and left in his hands (sometimes, but not often, this sparing of their lives was partly motivated by the hope of Rom. 11:26); or people felt themselves called to execute God's curse upon them. Precisely in relation to *this* minority problem, the moral and theological grounds are closely intertwined, either in such a way that theological arguments were made an excuse for anti-Jewish animosity, or else that they first elicited it, and it is precisely the latter possibility that burdens Christian statements about Judaism, especially after this terrible history, with special responsibility.

That is the reason why, since 1945, the hybrid manner of speaking about Judaism, which had so long been prevalent in Christian thinking and had spread not only among the Gentiles but also among their prominent thinkers, has almost disappeared. The horror at the holocaust was too great, and the feeling—at least half-conscious—of our complicity, was too painful for people to feel able to speak unhesitatingly as before. A minority of Christian theologians were further convinced that a renunciation of anti-Semitism, however forthright, was not enough, but that the anti-Jewish tradition in Christian theology and piety, which prepared the way for this modern anti-Semitism and which is to be found only among Christianized peoples, must be subjected to fundamental scrutiny. It must be asked if really negative judgments about Judaism are essential for the Christian faith, and whether, in consequence, the opposition between the two religions is as irrevocable as both sides have repeatedly claimed. This is an inquiry which we have not yet nearly completed; anyone who concerns himself with it is feeling his way in new territory which has surprises in store and calls old convictions into question. For it is an essential requirement that we set up this inquiry, not alone, in a Christian monologue, but together with the Jews in Christian-Jewish dialogue. In the new history of this dialogue since 1945 we have already experienced what, according to Martin Buber's "dialogic," is characteristic of a true conversation: both partners must make their deliberations together, neither must withhold his judgment from the other, and neither must evade the judgment of the other; no one must fix a program for the dialogue, but each must be ready for its surprises, and each must be ready to emerge from it changed.

How must a man speak of Judaism who speaks of Christianity? The source is Jewish, there can be no doubt about that. If the source, as we have seen, is continually the great question addressed to the stream, then the manner in which Christian theology speaks about Judaism concerns the relation of the stream to the source, and it is this which gives the theme so central a significance.

That the source is Jewish is in the first place historically incontestable: Jesus of Nazareth was a Jew. The first Christian post-Easter congregations with their missionaries, together with (all, or nearly all) the authors of the New Testament, were Jews. And the Holy Scripture of the Jews, the Hebrew Bible, was adopted by the Christian church as the first part of its canon, and that in a very deliberate manner, in rejection of Marcion's proposal[52] to purge the Gospels and the apostolic writings of all reference to the Old Testament.

In its first stage the Christian church was Jewish sect. This might have remained so, if a separation had not been compelled by two factors: that the Easter message about Christ is addressed "to all," and that thereby the "dividing wall" between Jews and non-Jews is broken down (Eph. 2:14) so that now the Gentiles also have access to God's covenant with Israel. This was soon realized in primitive Christianity (whether the mission to the Gentiles was already envisaged by the historical Jesus is debated). The success of the primitive Christian mission in the Mediterranean world, and the triumph of the Pauline principle that non-Jews, when they became Christians, were not to be subjected to the Mosaic law, led Christianity speedily beyond its limitation to Judaism. This process was accelerated by the rapidly stiffening opposition to the new group on the part of the Jewish majority, which finally led to their excommunication (in the prayer of the "Eighteen Benedictions").[53] This meant that a first door was slammed in the face of the expansion of the Christ faith in Judaism, to which was added the slamming of a second door by the persecution of the Jews by the Christians.

The result was, *not* the rise of a church consisting of Jews and Gentiles, such as Paul had envisaged, but its transformation into a Gentile Christian church (in which to the present day the few Jewish Christians have only the symbolic function of reminding us of the original constitution of the church as a community consisting of Jews and Gentiles). The schism between church and Israel was completed. This was a decisive new direction for the course of the stream of the Christian church; and later another equally momentous direction was added to it, when the Christian churches in Asia Minor and North Africa were destroyed by the attack of Islam, and the church, which had become Gentile Christian, consequently became also a church of the white race. Owing, however, to its connection with the source, the relationship with Judaism could not be repudiated, and it was impossible to establish Christianity as an entirely new religion. It remained a daughter religion of Judaism (even more so than the second daughter religion, Islam) and this has always caused the church and theology much difficulty. It also explains Christian irritability in relation to Judaism, which brought such disasters on the Jews who were at the mercy of the Christianized nations.

The difficulties showed themselves in the relation to

the Old Testament, and in the relationship to the historical Jesus, who, as a historical person and not as a mythical idea, remains the central event of which the Christian message speaks. Not only was he a real Jew, whose home was nowhere else than in the faith of Israel, he knew himself to be sent in the service of no other God than the God of Abraham, Isaac, and Jacob, and sent only "to the lost sheep of the house of Israel" (Matt. 15:24). Even the significance of his coming, his death and resurrection, could not be interpreted by the primitive Christian fellowship except with the help of the Old Testament, and as an action of the God of Israel—and, indeed, as the action which was the fulfillment of his own promises.

Friedrich Nietzsche has, however, described this as "that preposterous farce about the Old Testament" which Christianity "has staged": "I mean the attempt to pull the Old Testament from under the feet of the Jews, with the assertion that it contains nothing but Christian teaching, and belongs to the Christians as the true Israel."[54] (Nietzsche here refers to the story of the wager between Zundelfrieder and Zundelheiner in Johann Peter Hebel's "Schatzkästlein.") In fact, this was a prevalent tendency in the Gentile Christian church; it is evident as early as the letter of Barnabas: owing to their rejection of Jesus the Jews have either lost God's word or never rightly possessed it; now at any rate it belongs to us Christians. Similarly the Jews have lost their salvation; their covenant with God was always merely provisional, a promise of the new covenant with God which we Christians now enjoy as "The new Israel"—the new and true people of God.

This thesis of the disinheritance of Israel, which was held to be indispensable for the self-understanding of the church, and is still held by many to be so, has two versions, one more brutal and one more humane. The first one regards the Jews, because of the killing of Jesus and their continuing rejection of the Christian message even today, as thrust out of the covenant with God and given over to the curse of the wrath of God. The second, more modern form claims only—as the supposed opinion of Paul—that with the coming of Jesus the role of Israel in the history of salvation has come to an end, and the Jewish people have been "profaned" and "degraded" to the status of a people like all other peoples.

For the role of the Old Testament in the church, this had several possible consequences:

1. Some emphasized its subordination to the New Testament. Its relation to the latter is that of a shadow to the light (The Letter to the Hebrews); it is a preliminary to the revelation in Christ, and is made obsolete by the coming of the latter; its content is essentially law, and is replaced by the gospel, and what continues to be significant in it for Christians is to be discovered by an interpretation in the light of the New Testament.

2. Others conceded its true canonical standing, and attempts were made to harmonize the two Testaments by means of allegorical exegesis and by the importation of Christian elements. This attitude, today still widely held even in the Western Christian churches, is politically influential especially in the oriental church in Arab countries, where the transfer of Israel's promises to the church, and a spiritualizing interpretation of the Old Testament, have led to a denial of all legitimation of the Jewish appeal to the Hebrew Bible and the Jewish consciousness of election. The result has been also a denial of the Jewish assertion that the people and the land belong together, and a corresponding hostility to the state of Israel which finds here a theological justification for its claims.

3. It was also possible to proclaim a complete break with the Old Testament. The "German Christians" of the

Nazi period were not the first to do this; it was done in the new Protestantism of Schleiermacher and Harnack. In the Introduction to his *The Christian Faith*, Schleiermacher states the following doctrinal proposition (paragraph 12):

> Christianity does indeed stand in a special historical connection with Judaism, but so far as concerns its historical existence and its aim, its relations to Judaism and heathenism are the same.

In the same vein Adolf von Harnack in 1921 wrote the following sentences in his Marcion book:

> To repudiate the Old Testament in the second century was an error, which the great church was right to reject; to retain it in the sixteenth century was a fate from which the Reformation was not able to free itself. But to conserve it since the nineteenth century as a canonical source is the result of religious paralysis in the church.[55]

This means that the establishment of Christianity fundamentally as a new religion, independent and self-sufficient, open to all, equally ·distant from all, and equally near to all, only by historical accident nearer to the Jews, is a fact from which no inference to a nearness in substance may be drawn. For this reason—as the "German Christians" argued—the religious tradition of every people could become for every people its "Old Testament," a preliminary step to its Christianization as, for example, the Edda could become our Old Testament. Here it is significant that in that context Schleiermacher speaks only of the Old Testament, not of Jesus. Moreover, he likes to replace the name Jesus with the title Christ, which also became a name in the Christian tradition, a title which for Schleiermacher describes the Redeemer as the center of the Christian fellowship. We see from this how closely the question of the relation between Christianity and Judaism is connected with a central question of modern theology, the question concerning the relation between the historical Jesus and the Christ of the Christian message.

Now that we have thus sketched the problem as a problem of the Christian tradition, let us inquire about the phenomenon of Israel and ask whether—and if so, how far—it has not only a historical and accidental, but indeed an essential, connection with the Christian message. In Christian theology, in order to make things easier for themselves, people have tended to make a fundamental distinction between Israel and Judaism after the end of the Jewish state (through the two catastrophes of the destruction of Jerusalem in A.D. 70 and the suppression of the last great revolt of Bar-Cochba in A.D. 135). This too was only a consequence of the disinheritance thesis, the claim that, in contrast with Israel, we have to do in the case of Judaism with a new, different people. We shall not try to operate with this thesis. In contemporary Judaism we have Israel before us; the Jewish people did not cease to exist with its dispersion in the diaspora after the end of its state, but preserved itself with incomparable toughness through the centuries although the usual attributes of a people—common territory, common state, and common language—were, some of them wholly, some of them almost entirely, lost. Nor will we be able to take the easier way, of understanding Judaism only as a religious fellowship, but for our further reflection we must take seriously the self-understanding of the Jews, which insists upon the indissoluble togetherness of people and religion (and—as a third component—the land also!). Only then shall we be in sight of the real problem, and only then, too, will Christian-Jewish dialogue be possible. The latter is an aim that we shall never achieve if, as has so often happened, we as non-Jews claim to know better what the Jews are than do the Jews themselves.

This Judaism understands itself as a people identical and continuous with the Israel of the Old Testament, and just because it does this, it becomes in a peculiar way the theme of Christian theology. If we give up the daring attempt to amputate the New Testament from the Old Testament, and to understand Christianity as a new religion, and consequently also the God of Christian faith—like Marcion—as another God, severed from the God of Israel, nay, opposed to him, then we must take account of the fact that the Bible believes, the New Testament confirming it, that God's saving work with his self-destroying humanity begins with a call, the call of Abraham, and Abraham not as an individual; in Abraham it is his seed that is called, and it is with the seed promised to him, with the people of Israel, that the covenant is made. God's work of salvation thus begins with the establishment of a human group—not a society of like-minded persons, but a society related by physical descent, a clan. An old saying runs, *Christianus fit, Judaeus nascitur* ("One becomes a Christian, one is born a Jew").

Here is a major difficulty for us today; this seems to lead us back into archaic times and conceptions. The significance of descent grows less and less for modern man, through his mobility in society, through the small family which hardly retains the memory of its ancestors, through the growing predominance of international thinking over national thinking, through increasing loss of the mental reservations against race mixture. National Socialist racism appears in contrast as a last abortive attempt to recover the significance of descent. (It is just this which makes possible the demagogic and infamous comparison between Zionism and Nazism!) In the early times of humanity, descent was an essential category in the ordering of society, ethnically between the peoples, and feudally within the people. The individual was not thought of as an isolated individual, but as the product of and related to the collective, which made his individual life possible. And this collective was thought of as a unity of ancestors, contemporaries, and descendants, persisting through time. Of course this was connected with the stability of the method of production, which was handed down with few changes, together with its means of production, ways of life, and forms of law.

Like a fossil left over from these earlier times, the Jews persist into our own age; along with the Gypsies they are the toughest of racial stocks. It is indeed possible for single individuals to be lost through assimilation, and for new individuals to be added through religious conversion, a contingency to which Judaism was always open, and which at once led to integration into the racial stock. But Israel has always understood itself to be essentially a society sharing a common descent; the person who has a Jewish mother is a Jew. Admittedly, it is very important that the bond of common descent is not the only thing that holds Judaism together; this is clear from the disputes in the state of Israel as to whether a Christian or a Moslem with a Jewish mother is to be regarded as Jew. The common relationship to the God of Israel and the guidance for life given by him through the Torah, and the life-style derived from it, the *Halacha*, is (although many Jews have emancipated themselves from it wholly or in part) the other bond that holds Judaism together. And to it we must add in conclusion yet another external influence, anti-Semitism, which, insisting on the Jewish character of even very assimilated Jews, and thrusting them back into Judaism, is a negative symptom of the *mysterium Judaicum*. Essentially, as the possibility of conversion to Judaism shows, the constitution of Israel through the divine covenant takes priority over the fellowship by common descent; this is shown at the beginning in the origin of Israel, and in the union of racially diverse stocks under the covenant at Sinai, and it continues to have further historical results. Should there prove to be some truth in the thesis of Arthur Koestler[56] that a great part of the Ashkenazi Jews of the East are descendants of the Khazar people who went over to Judaism in the tenth century A.D., this would be an example of the power of integration which enabled the religion to incorporate into its racial fellowship not only, and repeatedly, many individuals but in this case a whole people.

If now, in our return to the source of the Christian faith, we come upon this peculiar people, the Jewish people, it cannot be a matter of indifference to us. At once we can draw from it two conclusions:

1. God's work of salvation begins with the creation of a human society, and indeed with the establishment of a people, and not with the revelation of new ideas, and also not with the gift of a prophetic book like the Koran. Judaism is primarily the Jewish people, the Jewish men and women in their togetherness as a people, integrated as a people by the covenant of God, and laid hold of from the beginning for that covenant.

2. This collective, characterized as a fellowship of common descent, though not exclusively so, is the beginning of God's new activity in the midst of his old self-destroying humanity, both by reason of its mere existence throughout history, but also as a "blind and deaf witness" (Isaiah 43!), *and* through its faith in God, *and also* by virtue of the nature of its social life. This means the renewal must happen through a real, new, social life, not only through a change in ideas, and not only through the change of individuals.

If the church has its source in Israel, then from this fact we may conclude that:

1. The church also is not meant to be merely a society of like-minded persons, much less an "invisible church" of dispersed people of similar faith, but to be a real life-fellowship.

2. In some way, still to be more precisely defined, the church belongs together with the real human society created before it by the same God whom it confesses, the Abrahamitic racial fellowship, the people of Israel.

For some this is hard to grasp, but it shows how closely Christian faith is connected with "accidental facts of history" (Lessing), and how hard it is to make faith universally visible. The case is entirely different from that of a complex of ideas deduced from principles universally self-evident. The indissoluble connection with Israel and the Jew Jesus of Nazareth, with such contingent historical facts, reminds us continually that in Christianity we have to do not with assent to definite doctrines, but with gratitude for concrete happenings in history, which are made known to us as God's intervening action.

The New Testament expresses this by the phrase "Since it has pleased God" (Gal. 1:15f.; Eph. 1:5). This means that choice has been made of certain facts of history. Men are given a destiny, and they do not escape from it; it determines their life and their history, it gives them a mission. The prophets, like Paul, know themselves chosen, from their mother's womb (Jer. 1:5; Gal. 1:15), and the birth stories of the New Testament wish to say the same for Jesus. This contradicts our modern conception of subjective autonomy, of the individual's right to self-determination. We ourselves choose what we wish to live for. Our consciousness of our own freedom—this must at once be emphasized in order to avoid a false antithesis—is not simply negated by the biblical concept of election, but it is certainly put within brackets. Election has power over us just as our birth, preceding our freedom, has power over us and in many ways determines the range of possibilities. But this power and determination does not cancel out our subjectivity as do the designation of a material and its formation as an instrument; it does not enslave a man, making him an *instrumentum animatum* ("a living instrument"), as the Romans called their slaves. Rather, the election of man to be God's messenger, God's witness, is the repetition of the original destiny of man, which is identical with his being, and does not alienate him from his being, but actualizes it. Man is created to be God's co-worker in the creation, and insofar as he is this, he fulfills the meaning of his existence. Israel is called, in the midst of a humanity that is failing to achieve its meaning, to be a new beginning of human meaningfulness, genuine humanity. This achievement of meaning is not compulsory, not mechanically necessary; it encounters the men concerned as a call and invitation of their creator, which they answer with the freedom given to them as men. I answer the choice which has caused me to become a man, not a beast. I answer it with my choice, with which I choose myself, with which I choose my destiny to be a man for God and for my fellowmen, and not a beast of prey in conflict with God and my fellowmen. Because we are part of lost humanity, there is a *special* choice of God to a *special* calling in connection with his work of salvation, but always directed to the good and salvation of all.

Election is thus anything but the arrogant self-exaltation of one man or one group above the rest. Admittedly, such misuse of even genuine election is possible, for those who are chosen are sinners! The Christian insolence of which we have spoken is a specially calamitous form of this misuse. Repeatedly within the history of Christianity individually Christianized peoples have sought aggrandizement by regarding themselves as successors of the chosen Israel. Within Israel itself the prophets were repeatedly forced to struggle against such a hybrid self-understanding. The real meaning of election is once and for all shown by the election of the man Jesus. He is chosen, not to judge, but to save. And this by giving his life to set free the others. Election is thus never an end in itself, but on the contrary a subordination to the others. Election is not aimed at the elect, but at the nonelect, who are to be helped by the elected one. In this sense the Christian fellowship, through its belonging to Jesus Christ, knows itself to be elected along with its Lord, and as such an elect church it must realize that earlier in time before it, and earlier than Jesus, the special election of God for the salvation of his human race began in the election of Abraham and Israel. Jesus did not first create his community, but came to his community when it was already prepared for him. Only as the "King of the Jews" is he the head of the body, and thus and only thus the salvation of the world. The Christian community is therefore an addition to the already existing community of Jesus, to God's community of Israel. The dividing wall is down (Eph. 2:14f.). Those who have been added from the Gentiles are yet another circle. The addition, and the removal of the dividing wall, does not destroy the special character of Israel. Those who come out of the Gentiles are called as individuals (*Christianus fit!*); and they constitute, together with those called to faith in Christ out of Israel, a sociologically different fellowship, constituted by baptism of the individual, alongside the racial fellowship of Israel (*Judaeus nascitur!*). The church is not a fellowship of racial descent, but "the people of the tongues of all the earth," as Luther says in his Whitsunday hymn.

It was, however, a false inference that was drawn in the church from this difference, i.e., that the church must take the place of the old people of God. With a horrified "By no means!" (*Me genoito*), Paul (Rom. 11:1) rejects such a line of thought, for that is the way in which he reacts to the question "Has God rejected his people?" which he has reformulated from the indicative of Ps. 94:14 ("The LORD will not forsake his people; he will not abandon his heritage"). Paul's absolute horror at such a

suggestion proves that the thought of God's breaking his
covenant with Israel was inconceivable to him. What
follows from this?

We see that, for Paul, since Christ, there are two
parallel communities of God, God's community Israel
and God's community the church. These two circles
intersect in the Jewish Christians, for they belong to both
of God's communities. Paul's hope is that one day—
when "the full number of the Gentiles" shall have found
entry to the realm of faith, and when Jesus Christ through
his appearing shall show who he is—"all Israel" will join
in the church's confession of Christ (Rom. 11:25f.). Paul's
present struggle was intended to ensure that Gentile
Christians are not compelled to become Jews, or to live
according to the Jewish law (a concern for which, according to Acts 15 he won the assent also of the other apostles
in Jerusalem). But he did not wish that Jews should stop
being Jews, or that the Jewish people should cease to
live according to the law that had been given to them.
Thus the Jewish people loses through the gospel of Jesus
Christ neither its existence nor its destiny to be, as a
people among the Gentiles, a witness to God in the life-
style of the people.

What is the meaning of this remarkable juxtaposition,
which is already a partial interfusion?

1. God's revelation to Israel, and the revelation of God
in Jesus directed to Israel as to all peoples, can be
claimed exclusively neither by Israel nor by the church;
but neither Israel nor the church can thrust one of these
revelations into the hands of the other as being of no
consequence to itself. For:

a. The Jesus event touches the Jews just as much as
the Gentiles; indeed, it touches them primarily: it is
primarily an event within Judaism. "Blessed be the Lord
God of Israel, for he has visited and redeemed his
people" (Luke 1:68). Jesus came first to the community
of Israel that had already been prepared for him. The

gospel is meant "for the Jews first" (Rom. 1:16), not in order that they should then go over to another new religion, but in order that every one of them might respond as "an Israelite indeed, in whom is no guile" to the call of Jesus, answering: "Rabbi, you are the Son of God, you are the King of Israel" (John 1:47–49). For this reason the evasion cannot be accepted which was proposed as early as Judah ha-Levi (1085–1141), and in our day by Franz Rosenzweig, Hans Joachim Schoeps, and other Jewish thinkers, that the message of Christ is not meant for the Jews, but opens for the Gentiles the door to the God of Israel.

b. The Old Testament belongs now also to the Gentiles, to the Gentile Christian church. It belongs to them with its promises as well as its command to renounce the silent, now-deposed gods, powers, and principalities, and to realize a life of society according to the will of God. Where—as in Catholicism and Calvinism—theocratic tendencies resulted from this, these must not be rejected wholesale, as signs of a decline into legalism. Their actual legalism consisted in the mechanical transference of Old Testament commands and instructions to a different national life in different times. But the element of truth in theocracy consists in the fact that God's will is valid, not only for the life of the individual but for the life of society, and therefore that we must seek to know it also in relation to political and social structures.[57]

2. Israel and the church, each in its particularity, belong indissolubly together. Augustine (354–430) gave a notable exposition of the parable of the two sons (Luke 15:11–32) in this sense. The elder son, Israel, is challenged to allow the opening of the covenant to the Gentiles, to accept them as brothers in the covenant (Rom. 15:7–13), to learn from them the freedom of God's kindness, to rejoice in them, and in fellowship with them. The younger son, the church, is challenged to be grateful to the elder brother, not to exalt itself arrogantly over

against him (Rom. 11:18), to let him live in the peculiar
manner that has been enjoined upon him, and to learn of
him, and with him.[58]

The first schism in the history of the church, the
schism between Christianity and Judaism, has been the
most disastrous for both parties. If we take seriously just
these Pauline thoughts about the difference and the
togetherness of the church and Israel, then it will be
clear to us that the ecumenical movement—and this is
unfortunately very far as yet from being clear to it—will
only be complete when it is also a movement of the
church toward the Jews, seeking new fellowship with
them.

3. Through the schism the Jews are suffering from the
absence of the Christians, and the Christians are suffering from the absence of the Jews.

a. The Jews are suffering from the absence of the
Christians. After Christ, the Jews heard the covenant
word apart from him whom many Jews call today their
"great brother" and their greatest prophet (Martin Buber,
Shalom Ben-Chorin, David Flusser, and others). The
Christians indeed bear their full measure of blame for
this. The result has been that the novelty of the Christ
event has not indeed been entirely excluded from Jewish
thought and life, but it has only penetrated feebly: the
freedom of the Spirit, the knowledge of love as the
original intention of the Torah, the justification of the
godless. There remains much rigidity, especially adher-
ence to the literal sense of the prescriptions of the
Halacha, without noting its tendency to a new social life,
as can be observed in the contemporary policies of
orthodoxy, and the national religious parties in the state
of Israel.

b. More important for us is the recognition that the
Christians are suffering from the absence of the Jews.
This absence has had such a profound influence on the
development of Christian theology as cannot here be

represented even in outline. In addition, it has had a similar effect as the contrary weakness among the Jews: namely, it has meant for Christians the separation of religion from the practical life of every day, especially from the life of society, the separation between Sunday and workdays, the attempt of the profane to declare its independence of God's will, supported by the individualizing and spiritualizing tendency of Christian preaching.

In the special theological field this is seen in the penetration of nonbiblical ways of thinking, as early as the formation of doctrine in the ancient church, and in the understanding of faith as assent to doctrine. Where this danger was recognized, and an attempt was made to recover the biblical understanding of faith (in Martin Luther, Albrecht Ritschl, Wilhelm Herrmann, Rudolf Bultmann), faith threatened to be enclosed within the realm of inner sentiment and narrowed down to its consolatory significance; the relation of faith to action, which was always the strength of Judaism, became insecure and was even in danger of being dissolved.

For this reason, in my opinion, the two dangers against which the two wings of the Reformation movement in the sixteenth century contended ought not to be regarded as equal. The difference between these two wings, the Wittenberg Lutheran and the Swiss Calvinist, can be described if we say that the Lutheran wing was concerned to prevent a Judaizing of the church, while the Calvinist wing was concerned to prevent its paganizing. But from what I have said about the relation of Israel and the church, it appears that we must not regard the dangers as equal. In the Christian proclamation the issue is that we "turn to God from idols to serve the living and true God" (I Thess. 1:9). The heathen nature, which is deeply rooted in us, and which ever and again perverts the church, consists in this, that we fear and love all sorts of other things more than the living God, that besides him we have many gods. Church history confirms how this heathen nature ever and again comes to the surface in the ties that bind the church to the powers that dominate contemporary society. The Jewish method of segregation from heathendom, which is based on the Torah, has not been imposed on us Gentile Christians, thanks to Paul, but neither have we any right to deny it to the Jews, or any license to neglect in our own way to keep ourselves pure from heathenism and to fight against its temptations. Neither for us nor for the Jews can this obedience to the First Commandment be a "way of salvation" with which we should deserve blessedness. ·The supposition that it is such for the Jews, and that for this reason we have to reject their bond to the Torah, is one of the anti-Jewish legends in Christian theology which must once and for all be refuted. The danger of "Judaizing," against which the Lutheran Reformation set its face, the danger of legalistic works righteousness, had spread far in the medieval church and still continues to be a threat. It is also a threat, of course, in Judaism, but it is *not* identical with careful observance of the Torah, with the strict *Halacha* of orthodox Judaism. Because this false identification is easy, the expression "Judaizing" for this danger should be dropped, and the idea that the genuine Christian way runs between heathenism and Judaism as the two seductive powers on the right and the left should be abandoned. This idea is a misinterpretation of the Jew Paul, and it is an obstacle to the new brotherly relation of Christians and Jews which, after too long a history of guilt, it is our task to create today.

RECOMMENDED READING

Christen und Juden. Eine Studie des Rates der Evangelischen Kirche in Deutschland. 1975. In addition: *Arbeitsbuch zur Studie: Christen und Juden.* 1979.

Geis, Robert Raphael. *Gottes Minorität. Beiträge zur jüdischen Theologie und zur Geschichte der Juden in Deutschland.* 1971.

Geis, Robert Raphael, and Kraus, Hans-Joachim (eds.). *Versuche des Verstehens. Dokumente jüdisch-christlicher Begegnung aus den Jahren 1918–1933.* Theologische Bücherei, No. 33. 1966.

Kraus, Hans-Joachim. *Begegnung mit dem Judentum. Das Erbe Israels und die Christenheit.* Furche-Stundenbücher, No. 16. 1963.

Marquardt, Friedrich Wilhelm. *Die Entdeckung des Judentums für die christliche Theologie. Israel im Denken Karl Barths.* 1967.

Pfisterer, Rudolf. *Von A bis Z. Quellen zu Fragen an Juden und Christen.* 1971.

Ruether, Rosemarie. *Nächstenliebe und Brudermord. Die theologischen Wurzeln des Antisemitismus.* Abhandlungen zum christlich-jüdischen Dialog, Vol. 7. 1978. (E. T. *Faith and Fratricide: The Theological Roots of Anti-Semitism.* Seabury Press. 1974.)

von der Osten-Sacken, Peter (ed.). *Treue zur Thora. Beiträge zur Mitte des christlich-jüdischen Gesprächs. Festschrift für Günther Harder zum 75. Geburtstag.* 1977.

VIII   The Kingdom
of God

The heart of the gospel, and therefore of the Christian faith, is the message of the Kingdom of God. The expression "Kingdom of God" means the victory of the gracious will of God over all opposing forces. God's will intends the good life of man, even now, under the provisional conditions of our present life, looking forward to the coming consummation.

What is the heart of the Christian faith? What is its goal, and in what does it already participate? By the different answers that have been given to this question in the course of Christian history, it can be seen how the message of Christ has appealed from time to time to different men and to different ages, and how people have sought to include the whole of this message, and consequently the whole of the Bible, under the particular aspect that had been vouchsafed to them.

The Augustinian theology—following the promise of Matt. 5:8—had named the *visio beata*, the vision of God of the blessed. The Augsburg Confession gives as the key to the Scriptures, and therefore also as the heart of the faith, the forgiveness of sins. For one great tradition of the Reformation theology, from Martin Luther to Ernst Käsemann, the justification of the godless is the great central divine miracle. Pietism named and names conversion, i.e., the renewal of man through the total surrender of one's own will to the will of God, or through personal communion of man with Jesus. Fichte found the blessed life in the union of man and God. Hegel found the consummation in knowledge: in the knowledge of the human spirit the Absolute Spirit returns to the knowledge of itself. The Christian mystics of all ages saw the door open to the transcendence of the dualism between man and God, to the *unio mystica* between the finite and the infinite. Many others found this perspective too speculative or world-denying; they found the most important thing in the gospel the command to love—in the injunction to change life in this world to a life of neighborly love, nay, of love to enemies, that overcomes evil with good.

All of these, insofar as each one of them takes up a persistent theme of the biblical writings, are true answers. Their limitation lies in the fact that by each of them the different major parts of the Bible—the historical books, the prophets, the Wisdom sayings, the Synoptic Gospels, John, Paul—are in each case given a different emphasis, in part become more prominent, in part less so. We are not able to take it upon ourselves to escape altogether the subjective and time-conditioned nature of our hearing, but if the answer is to be as little subjective and as far as possible just to the whole of the biblical message, then it appears to me that the central concept of the preaching of Jesus is at the same time the most biblically comprehensive. Within it, these other partial answers emphasize parts and elements. Hence the thesis: The Kingdom of God is the theme of the Bible and the heart and core of the Christian faith.

In German, the expression "Kingdom of God" is misleading. It suggests spatial and material associations because "kingdom" (*Reich*) refers to areas on the geographical map, or to historical constitutional conditions. One thinks of the end of the Holy Roman Empire of the German people, or of the contemporary question of the continuation of the German Empire after 1945. The expression must be given an active and dynamic quality from its Hebrew background. In Hebrew, *malkuth*

YHWH is to be understood primarily in a verbal sense: God's rule; only secondarily does the expression mean the condition and sphere of this rule.

When the Gospel of Matthew speaks in Greek of the "Kingdom of Heaven," not only does it follow the Jewish injunction to avoid, out of reverence, the name of God, and the word "God," but it refers also to different realms of the divine rule.

1. There are realms in which God already rules without opposition. These are the "heavens," the world of the angels (cf. the third petition of the Lord's Prayer).

2. There is (and this is, moreover, very paradoxical, and therefore inconceivable for a monistic believer in God like Spinoza!) another realm in which God is already *de jure* Lord, and indeed rules as its Creator, but does not rule *de facto* without opposition, but in conflict with strong opposition, and therefore in a concealed manner and in such a way that he and his rule are not directly perceptible, not yet visible "face to face." That is the earth, in particular the world of men.

3. This is a "not yet" situation: God's reign in the full sense is only present where it has achieved a complete victory, where there is no longer any contradiction, where even the "last enemy," death, is overcome (I Cor. 15:26; cf. Rev. 21:4), and where "face to face" we thank him without reserve for his rule (I Cor. 13:12).

History is moving toward this reign of God, not because of its own teleology, but because it is creation history, the history of the creation of the world, which is wrongly conceived so long as it is not thought of as creation confronting its Creator. The victory of the Creator's will in overcoming all opposition—that is the eschatological event to which biblical prophecy looks forward, possibly from a very early stage of the faith of Israel (cf. Gen. 12:1–3); then it is the dominating theme in the prophets and for Jesus. The various religions are customarily concerned with the interpretation and the ordering of the cosmic process, with which the ordering of society is made to correspond: the eternity and immutability of norms and ordinances, and a dependable repetition of the cosmic rhythm. If in religion and metaphysics the cosmos is transcended, this gives access to a world above and behind this world, into which we can ascend out of the transitory world of appearance—as in the high religions of Asia and in ancient metaphysics. But here, in biblical eschatology, transcendence is directed to the future. This means that criticism of the present condition of the world is not its denial (in the sense of an escape into a higher sphere), but is indeed its affirmation as creation: now alienated, in contradiction, and inauthentic but, thanks to the constancy of its Creator, moving toward its authentic nature, its true created identity.

This great hope for the future does not look out into an abstracted futurity. Already God rules in the midst of the contradiction, through his concealed action and his revealed spoken word. His word, which can already be heard, is the central eschatological fact of the present. For this reason God's rule is always to be spoken of as belonging to the future and to the present; that is true of the prophets, but even more so of Jesus. The man who now lets God rule in his life is a witness to the future in which "the earth shall be filled with the glory of the LORD" (Num. 14:21), and he shares in working for this future. Upon the victory of God in his creation, over all opposition, both in the individual and in the universe, *everything* in biblical faith depends.

But all these expressions are still too formal. It could still for that reason be conceived in a very heteronomous manner as the setting up of a totalitarian rule, the despotism of a transcendent superego propagated by people who, in some future or present way, wish to share in the profit by subjecting men to their own rule and by participating in the totalitarian rule of God. In the thousand years of a society of privilege, the conception of rule has been so discredited as a concept of selfishness and expropriation of others by feudal and hierarchical authorities that it needs purification before it can express what faith intends by it; indeed, it needs a purification as radical as that which Jesus effected by his cross, where the royal entry—travestied by the ass, the crown of thorns, the bamboo scepter, and the inscription on the cross—points forward to the reversal of the previous meaning of rule.

So what does God's rule look like? What is the content of the Kingdom of God? How can God's rule be hope for us? Only, to be sure, if and when our life in the Kingdom of God is not the life of contented slaves, satisfied by security and adequate maintenance, but cheated of their own life, their own being. Only, to be sure, if and when in this kingdom we experience not the expropriation but the appropriation of real life, when in it with God we ourselves come to our goal, when in it that is destroyed which destroys us, when the rule of God is identical with our own free life.

What was intended in the chapter on God can here for the first time be made clear. What the Bible means by "God" is defined biblically by the content of the promise of the Kingdom of God. The biblical experience sees directed to every one of us—to the whole of humanity, to the smallest as well as to the greatest human life—an *affirmation* coming out of eternity, a stream of help, an inexhaustible solidarity and an endless and tireless endeavor to help us to achieve life. The victory of the rule of God is identical with the triumph of this endeavor.

"God" in the biblical sense is the most positive thing that can be said about us men. "God" is a word of promise and hope: eternity *for* and not against us men of time. When the two accounts of creation (Genesis 1 and 2) are so read, there emerges one overarching theme from the beginning to the end of the Bible: "Behold the dwelling of God is with men, and he will dwell with them, and they shall be his people, and he himself, God with them, shall be their God" (Rev. 21:3).

In the world of the religions this existence of God *for* men is anything but taken for granted. There may be gods who are only harmful to men. Fundamentally, every god can become useful or harmful to man, according to whether man succeeds in winning his favor or not. Here—in the symbolism of mythological personal relationship—there is a reflection of our whole life. It is a system of conditions upon which our survival depends, either through achievement, buying the favor of the mighty ones, or through winning the power of life (mana) by devices, or through luck (i.e., the accidentally favorable constellation of a fate neutral to us). Always insignificant man lives through his success in so fitting himself in with higher plans that while he is used for these, he at the same time makes his own profit, man for the gods!

The approach of God to us which is experienced by biblical faith is our elevation out of this system of conditions by unconditional affirmation that (1) creation is grace; (2) creation is not yet complete, but is on the way to still greater glory; (3) creation is a fight against all obstacles to salvation, preservation, and consummation of the creature in the Kingdom of God.

Now one thing ought to be clear about the triumph of God's will: it is not achieved at our expense; it does not mean that we are used up for alien purposes; rather, it is identical with the fulfillment of *our* life. This is the design suggested in the Old Testament. In the New Testament this is so clear that what precedes appears as a promise, because the covenant has now advanced to

become self-identification of the Lord of the covenant
with the covenant partner. This is the source of the New
Testament certainty and joy, this intimacy between man
and God, this simultaneity of being already at the goal
and being still on the way there.

But what is fulfillment of life, what is the good and the
true life? Here it can come to a difference between the
divine and the human will, to an apparent heteronomy of
the divine will. The question is whether *we* can take for
granted our knowledge of what "the good life" is. It
could indeed be that we mistake what is false, what is
deadly, for what is good. There is all the more danger of
this since the distinction between the true and the false,
between the good and the bad life, is by no means in
reality decided from the throne of our moral independence, from the tribunal of the autonomous reason, as
would appear from the writing of some philosophers. In
reality our opinions are profoundly influenced by what
our neighbors around us consider to be the good life. We
are not free; we have first to be set free to make an
independent judgment with which we can confront critically the value systems that prevail in our society.

What did the majority of Germans in the days of
Wilhelm II, on the way toward the times of Hitler, and
finally in the days of Hitler, believe to be the good life?
What does the normal white citizen in South Africa
consider it to be? Or, to take an example nearer home: In
the schools of the Federal Republic of Germany the
scholars are trained by the examination system to behave
in a competitive manner. Through the forcing in of
examinable information they are compelled to compete
with their fellow students to win an entrance to university studies. As a place for the production of asocial go-
getting egoists, such a school is only a mirror of the
society that needs them. In capitalistic society the entrepreneur is compelled to create increased productivity
and accumulate profit in order to achieve growth, if he is

not to go under, and the worker is compelled to direct his power as a worker according to the requirements of his employers, in order to defeat the competing worker, in order himself not to land on the scrap heap of unemployment. At the same time we are all drilled to seek for our quality of life in the quantity of private consumption, even when this is done at the cost of the infrastructure of society and the life resources available for all. These are forms peculiar to capitalism of the perennial conviction that, in the face of the scarcity of the means of life available to society, everyone must seek his advantage at the expense of the others; that privileges are given to us in order to claim advantages; and that the good life consists in getting privileges before others. The society that is hierarchically built up on privilege is the result of this conviction, and it perpetuates itself by so indoctrinating this conviction through its very structure, by means of socialization in all its members, that another form of society is hardly thinkable, indeed is feared rather than sought for.

Men are so deformed by the stamp set on them by society that they become incapable of another life. We are so deformed by the capitalist society, by its specific form of life at the expense of others, that we become incapable of living in a genuinely socialist society, incapable of even wishing it. At the best we think of it as a beautiful dream without reality. Indeed, we thereby betray a suspicion that that "good life" which is won in a murderous fashion, i.e., at the cost of other life, is not really the good life, on which everything depends, but that this really good life is unfortunately only a dream.

The Bible calls this opposition of the present conception of the good life to the really good life *sin*. The instances of the specific deformation of our striving for the good life in our present (dis)order of society show two things:

1. Sin is at the same time our own action and our

failure, and a failure that rules over us. The Marxian dialectic is right: society is at the same time the product of men and of the power that rules over men. What society impels me to will is at the same time my own will, and this will, which is the will of all of us, objectifies itself as society's compulsion over us. For this reason, change in the social order which stems from this will is by itself not enough; so long as we are not freed from this will we shall again pervert even a better order, e.g., a socialist one, into a system of privilege. Liberation on both sides would have to be achieved, in the general will of society and in the particular will of the individual. How is such liberation achieved?

2. The false will, which regards the false life as good, has its deepest root in our trusting only ourselves. We mistrust the other person, and we mistrust everything that we call "God," fate as well as the great powers, and all this we do with good reason—or rather, with bad reason. They all belong to the system of conditions in which we can only preserve our life by asserting ourselves and securing an advantage over the rest.

This situation is totally changed when we hear the eternal affirmation (because this affirmation, which transcends everything else, alone deserves to be called "God"), when we accept ourselves and believe we are accepted. That is liberation, to realize that the good life consists in something other than self-assertion and privileges. Not to believe in God's "Yes," not to trust in his love—that is the reason for our false will and our false conception of life. Unbelief is the real sin (Luther).

From this it becomes clear also that I can become a sinner in the true sense only when encountered by the word of affirmation, opposing to it my mistrust; that is, only in the realm where the love of God is proclaimed. For this reason in the Bible the place of genuine, impossible, senseless, unforgivable sin—and therefore sin only removable by the *miracle of forgiveness*—is this realm, Israel, the disciple band, the Christian community, and not the outside world.

What has been said can be confirmed by a study of the biblical text and will demonstrate itself as the universal viewpoint of that text—not as a borrowing from modern humanism, but, on the contrary, as the fundamental tradition from which this humanism stems and that on which, if well advised, it can nourish itself.[59] For our inquiry about the *content* of the promise of the Kingdom of God, the result is as follows:

1. However great may be the contrast between "God's will and our wishes,"[60] God's will is basically a will in man's favor, not hostile, and not indifferent to men. This makes it a will which can be the ground of promise and hope for men.

2. The good life which is the goal of this will consists of the double relationship to God and to men; it is *fellowship*, removal of isolation, of loneliness and self-centeredness; indeed, it is fellowship with God. Now, because of the hidden nature of the divine working, it consists in faith, i.e., trust in God's word of promise which casts out fear and the self-interest that takes no thought of others—but in the consummation it will be vision face to face (I Cor. 13:12). In the same way it is relationship with others; since faith sets us free from fear, it sets us free for those from whom fear and self-seeking separate us.

3. Because fear and self-seeking also destroy our relation to nature, changing this from keeping the garden (Genesis 2) to a ruthless exploitation, the Bible also points to a healing of the relation to nature, and has therefore a cosmic perspective.

4. Biblical faith is eschatological, i.e., it regards history as God's progress in his project of perfecting his still-unfinished creation and of restoring the wandering, self-

destroying human race to their salvation.

5. The story of Jesus Christ, toward which the story of the covenant with Israel points, is the coming of God into his world. "God comes in Israel to the world"[61] in a double sense. His covenant with Israel is the coming of the promise of his Kingdom for the whole world. And he comes in Jesus in Israel to the world, as a man comes into the world; in this man he is present as a part of his world to this world of his, setting up his rule in it in a most secret but irrevocable manner. From this point God reaches out to the whole of humanity, laying hold of its actual state and condition in revolutionary fashion, with a view to the complete victory of his rule, the ultimate Kingdom of God. This is the source of the consciousness of novelty, and the consciousness of already participating in the goal, which fills the primitive Christian church in its confrontation with Judaism.

6. Through the story of Jesus Christ that was enacted on earth, the Kingdom is thus already present, and at the same time belongs to the future. The Kingdom is a hidden reality, which directs those who are drawn into it by the word and faith to look eagerly into the future; it sets them free, through forgiveness, for the future; and it commits them to serve the future of mankind.

7. God's project for the victory of his rule (i.e., his will for mankind) shows what the good life is. It does this in the challenge to us that makes known this will—i.e., the commandments, whose heart is the twofold command-ment of love, as the answer to God's self-sacrifice for his human race. Hence the saying, "Whoever would save his life will lose it, and whoever loses his life for my sake will find it" (Matt. 16:25), and the Golden Rule (Matt. 7:12; Rom. 12:9–21). That is the *metanoia* ("repen-tance") which focuses upon the Kingdom of God which has broken in upon our world with Jesus. The apostolic *paraineseis* ("exhortations") describe the life of the com-

munity as the life of a cell of the new society experiencing in anticipation the Kingdom of God under the conditions of the old age, and in the midst of the old age. For the Kingdom of God does not mean only individual fellowship with God in the transcendent world (heaven) but *a new social life*. Martin Buber is right when he says:

> What he [Jesus] calls the Kingdom of God—however it may be determined by a feeling of the end of the world and a sense of wonderful transformation—is, for all that, no sense of consolation in the beyond, no vague heavenly blessedness, nor is it spiritual or cultic association, nor a church; it is the perfect life of men together, it is the perfect fellowship, which, just for that reason, is the immediate reign of God, his *basileia*, his earthly kingdom.[62]

8. The community lives in this new social life, not as an island (monastery) of enclosed persons, but as light, salt, and leaven that work outward (Matt. 5:13–16; 13:33), both through its proclamation and through the active pursuit of the other life, the good life. By its means, the message of the Kingdom of God is even now the critical challenge and attack of the Kingdom of God, launched against an evil, godless life, both in the life of the individual and, because it is a social life, in society.

9. The outreach of this activity undertaken by Christians as individuals, and by the community as a whole, also has a dimension of political responsibility, i.e., in influencing the social and political order and the laws of the state, not as a special political party, but—as befits their mission to the world—within the political and social groupings in cooperation with non-Christians, whatever may be the motives and philosophical principles that inspire the latter in their pursuit of the same concrete goals of the day. The criterion for such cooperation is accordingly not the Christian conviction of the

others, but the question whether in their motivation they also are moving in the same "line and direction"[63] which the message of the Kingdom of God has assigned to the Christian sense of responsibility for the world: *better* communal life, i.e., a world order which better than any other serves the "liberty, equality, and fraternity" of men.

10. The comparative term ("better") which has just been used results from the "eschatological reserve" under which the life and work both of Christians and of grace stand in the world. They live under the conditions of the old age, which they cannot remove, and which still continue to influence them also, namely, *guilt* and *death*. The removal of these is the work of the great revolution, the great liberation of the Kingdom of God, which only God can accomplish. It is already accomplished where, through the Holy Spirit, men are set free from bondage to themselves and from the fear of death, for faith and love. This present work of the Kingdom of God makes us a battlefield between our inclination toward the old life of death and our liberation for the new, good life.

What this means for political responsibility is that we cannot make the *absolute utopia* of the Kingdom of God our program, but we can make our program the *concrete utopia* of a society still stamped by sin and death, yet one more just and free, that is, a classless society—a society no longer torn asunder into classes with opposing interests. The approximation to this is the criterion for Christian participation in political life. Thus even the earthly goal is this fundamentally revolutionary opposition to the unfree, unequal, unbrotherly society in which we live— quite apart from the question whether the approximation can be made in small steps, by evolution or reform, or in one great step by revolution. Thus advocacy of the cause of the most thoroughgoing movement in the struggle for social justice and political freedom is a part of the political responsibility of the Christian fellowship,[64] and indeed this must always be a *critical* advocacy, for both in our case and in the case of the others with whom we cooperate, we still have to do with persons who are deeply influenced by the conditions of the old age, and are always in need of new liberation. Therefore we shall have to face a permanent revolution,[65] i.e., a *movement* toward the concrete utopia, a constantly renewed reduction of new possibilities of privilege and the rule of privilege—not in order to reach a condition that is the earthly reflection of the Kingdom of God, but as a movement of endless approximation (even insofar as the concrete utopia is concerned) toward the continual and active fulfillment of the second petition of the Lord's Prayer: "Thy will be done on earth as it is in heaven."

RECOMMENDED READING

Kraus, Hans-Joachim. *Reich Gottes—Reich der Freiheit. Grundriss systematischer Theologie.* 1975.

Stähli, Martin. *Reich Gottes und Revolution. Christliche Theorie und Praxis für die Armen dieser Welt.* Die Theologie des religiösen Sozialismus bei Leonhard Ragaz und die Theologie der Revolution in Lateinamerika. 1976.

Tillich, Paul. *Systematic Theology,* Vol. 3. University of Chicago Press, 1963.

IX   Grace and Gratitude

"The Kingdom of God" means the presence of grace and the promise of the victory of grace. God's grace seems to stand in opposition to human freedom. Rightly understood, however, grace is the gift of freedom for activity. The freedom that grace gives is the freedom of gratitude. Gratitude for grace is cooperation with God for the purpose of the divine enterprise of salvation.

In Chapter VIII we spoke of the promise or the message of the Kingdom of God. But even this makes it clear that God's enterprise of salvation, the victory of his reign in favor of a life that is really good for us, is not an enterprise that leaves us, who are now living, out of account, or that takes place over our heads, or that miraculously, at the end of history, in one stroke replaces this world by another world—a world purely of the future, having no connection with our life today. If that were so, it would not need to be proclaimed, or else its proclamation today would be nothing but consolation in our present misery. It would only give us the prospect of a future transformation for good about which we can rejoice because a share in it is promised to us after our death and in spite of our death, without its having any transforming influence upon our life today in our present misery.

Such a reduction of the promise of the Kingdom of God to an *eschaton* in the beyond—whether far or near—has often happened in the Christian tradition, and we can hear of it even today. Class interests as well as philosophical prejudices have played a part in this. The intellectuals who came into the church in the first centuries brought to it their conception of the immutability of the cosmos and of the corresponding fundamental order of

154

the life of society, and with it also their need for elevation above the prison of this cosmos into a kingdom of
pure Spirit.[66] The challenge, revolutionary for society, to
live here and now a changed life corresponding to the
Kingdom of God thus fell into the background; eschatology became a last hope of the pious, directed to the
beyond, and in theology became the "Doctrine of the
Last Things." The actual society of the day, with its class
domination, was thereby protected from the critique of
the proclamation of the Kingdom of God; thus when
oppressed classes of the population took up this critique
again, and when they found in it a justification of the
challenge for social change, this could be opposed in the
name of the now-orthodox eschatology as "enthusiastic"
or "chiliastic" heresy. The official eschatology became
an ideological weapon against actual interpretation of the
message of the Kingdom of God as significant for this
world.

But such significance for this world can only be removed from this message by very far-fetched arguments.
For this reason it has a continually disturbing effect, and
it is repeatedly cited by those who have in a special
degree to suffer the distress of present misery, in order to
demand that changes should be made now. However
much error may have crept in from time to time, this is
justified by the fact that the proclamation of the Kingdom
of God is meant to awaken the hope of the complete
victory of the will of God in order to achieve a transformation of life here and now. In the summary of the whole
of Jesus' preaching this is unmistakably clear: "Repent,
for the kingdom of heaven is at hand" (Matt. 4:17).

I sum up this repentance under two headings, *grace*
and *gratitude*. This may be surprising, because universally the word "gratitude" refers to a change of life to be
made from our side as human beings, but not so, apparently, the word "grace."

The reaction to the word "grace" reveals the modern

alienation of the use of language in the church from its use outside the church. However central its use in the church may be, and however glad people are to hear it and to use it, this word can elicit violent rejection among outsiders. To them it sounds like a feudal leftover, reminding them of the obsequious address "Gracious Sir" or "Gracious Madam." Grace appears as an attitude of condescension. The word emphasizes the dependence of the subordinate. In the sociopolitical field the workers have replaced dependence on the grace of the factory owner—which is always uncertain, and where uncertainty emphasizes their dependence—by legal relations which can be the subject of action at law. We do not wish to live by the grace of others, but by what we can claim as our right. In order to educate the workers to uphold stoutly the struggle for their rights, Marxism has set its face in strict opposition to the church's doctrine of grace, even in the deepest philosophical questions of creation and historical evolution, and has opposed to it the thesis of the self-creation of man through labor:

> A being only appears independent when it stands on its own feet, and it only stands on its own feet when it owes its existence to itself. A man who lives by the grace of another regards himself as a dependent being. But I live completely by the grace of another when I owe to him not only the maintenance of my life: but when in addition to this he has created my life, when he is the source of my life; and my life has necessarily such a ground external to itself when it is not its own creation. The creation is therefore a conception very hard to expel from the popular consciousness. The independent status of nature and of man is inconceivable to it, because it contradicts all the tangible evidence of practical life.[67]

Here Marx stands in the tradition of the modern revolt against grace, which extends from Renaissance humanism through the Enlightenment to the modern non-Marxist forms of contemporary achievement ideology. Only through his own efforts can man give his existence a meaning, which he can obtain from no other source. He has only himself to thank for what he is, and for what meaning he achieves in life. This admittedly very precarious dependence on oneself is, however much it robs him of all other supports, his distinctive character, which he must on no account surrender for any heteronomy of contented slavery.

However, in this antithesis of autonomous freedom and heteronomous dependence on grace there is reflected an antithesis which was always present in the church's theology of grace. It rests upon the apparent antithesis, in which the Bible, in different statements, now makes everything depend on the free decision and achievement of man, and now makes everything depend on the divine grace, an antithesis which became especially manifest in the conflict between Erasmus of Rotterdam[68] and Martin Luther,[69] with their appeal on both sides to Holy Scripture. But it had already become evident in the conflict between Pelagius and Augustine, and in the conflict between the Lutheran and the Tridentine doctrines of grace it received stable expression as the conflict between two Christian confessions, Lutheranism and Roman Catholicism. The two theses stood in unreconciled opposition: *Either* man is responsible, and therefore a free being; and then in the decisive point, in relation to God and his salvation, he is himself the author of his own fortune. *Or* man confronts God in absolute dependence, as the word "God" taken seriously in its biblical significance challenges us to think; and then everything is grace, and man in decisive matters is passive. *Either* man owes his salvation to himself *or* he owes it to God. The mediating attempts made by the scholastic and Erasmian doctrine of grace—which sought as it were to reckon the share of God and the share of man in percentages, in order to be fair to both—could not overcome the sharp antithesis, but only obscured it. For, however minimal one may judge the share of man to be, if it really depends on him, then his contribution is in the last resort decisive and salvation in the last resort is self-salvation—for which man has to thank himself, in contradiction to gratitude to God *alone*, which undeniably the Bible consistently demands of man.

Where such antitheses appear, they stimulate human thought, even in theology, to ask the question whether we are here confronted by a final contradiction. Is this a case of truth against falsehood? Can the two conflicting convictions only encounter each other with the last desperate alternative of confession and repudiation, each of them understanding itself as the position of faith against unbelief?

It could be that this is the case. But this possibility must not hinder us from testing whether we have not here a cul-de-sac of thought, from which by renewed weighing of the premises and concepts an escape, a transcendence of the antithesis, can be found. It seems to me to be the epochal significance of Karl Barth for Christian theology to have achieved this examination and to have found a way out. His theology is a theology of the divine grace and a theology of human freedom in one, without embarking on these attempts at mediation, with their merely apparent transcendence of the antithesis.

Barth repeats without modification the radical character of the Reformation teaching on grace, and he discloses more clearly than the latter that grace is the source of human freedom—indeed, that human freedom is a way in which grace, rightly understood, operates. This indeed he does only through more precise questioning as to what really is to be understood by "freedom," and when we really might be able to describe ourselves as "free indeed" (John 8:36).

Let us first remain on the human plane, and ask whether the modes of speech of the antigrace faction describe our reality. To owe everything to oneself, and not to live from the grace of others—not even a Robinson Crusoe could speak thus, let alone one of us who live in a manifold and indissoluble relationship with society. "One remains a debtor to others for what one is."[70] That is obvious. We cannot escape our dependence on the grace of others. It is well known that Martin Niemöller said that the question people ask today is no more "How do I find a gracious God?" but "How do I find a gracious neighbor?" With that the word "grace" is already defeudalized and generalized. Repeatedly, someone near me will in some respect be stronger than I am, and will have the power of cutting my life-arteries—either an individual facing me as an individual, or as a person in power, or a group of people in power, confronting me as a member of my social collective, through economic pressure, politics, war, etc. Will that more powerful person, will these powerful people, be inclined to do the contrary, to grant me life, not to set their power in motion to destroy me? Will they be gracious and merciful to me? No pride should prevent me from seeing the continuing actuality of this question!

But does this mean that the question "How do I find a gracious God?" is out of date? In this historical formulation it beset the young Luther as a man of the late Middle Ages, and when he was liberated from it by new knowledge of the gospel, the Middle Ages in him were subdued. But what the question means reaches far beyond this historical epoch and touches what is universally human.

"God" means here the last horizon of our being, its first and last conditioning frame of reference. Is he gracious, or ungracious? That question arises when the lack of grace is certain, or at the least possible. We have experience of the "gracious neighbor," his friendly approach, his mercy, tolerance, and love in the field of human relationships. Can such experience make that question unnecessary?

To even the most enriching experience of love we may at once add two other experiences:

a. We experience the fact that our human love is limited; this includes the love of others for us as well as our love for others. All our loving is defective; no one loves his neighbor as himself.

b. We find that our love is not only qualitatively but quantitatively limited: by time, which can bring about the loss of the loved person in many ways, through separation, through death, but also through different development, by estrangement. We love for a time, but our love is unprotected, it is limited by an ungracious horizon. Love between human beings is—as it appears to us often enough—a threatened, isolated phenomenon, a solitary beautiful flower, an edelweiss in a world of crag and ice.

The horizon can be described in two ways: the horizon of nonbeing and the horizon of guilt. Instead of nonbeing we may say death, fate, nature, the universe—anything that will again engulf us, the vast indifference around us as ground for our anxiety. By human love we are protected from this; we can for a moment forget it, and we are secure in this forgetfulness. But this makes us more vulnerable in our secret knowledge of the possibility, nay, the certainty of its loss someday. Love casts out our fear for the time being—*and* makes us more fearful than when in our loneliness we have only to look after ourselves.

The horizon of *guilt* too is without grace. When our guilt is heavy, we build up a protective wall by means of self-excuse (minimizing our guilt; exculpating ourselves by appeal to determining circumstances; justifying our actions in the face of those whom we have sacrificed, by referring to our exalted ends). The conception of a Last Judgment, which is to be found not only in the Bible but universally among all nations, means that someday these walls will collapse, someday the people we have sacrificed and forgotten, whom we have shouted down by our self-justification, the victims of our action and (still more) of our neglect, will confront us face to face with their questions and accusations. Someday our anxious question will be addressed to these sacrifices of our life, who remorselessly present their accusations: "How do I find a gracious neighbor?" And it will be identical with the question "How do I find a gracious God?" Someday we shall no longer be able to conceal and excuse ourselves.

Dies irae, dies illa ("Day of wrath, that dreadful day") . . .[71] It is most inadvisable to write this off as primitive, to think that all this can be explained away as fear cunningly drilled into us by a stern superego, used by the ruling class to hold the people down. It is better to take this seriously as the expression of an awareness of our infinite responsibility for our life, an inescapable question and indictment, which cannot be canceled out like a debt by the production of our other good works. It is the inevitably impending hour of truth, from which not even death can rescue us, because even if there were no life after death, no hell, and if death merely annihilates me, nevertheless the question and accusation brings in a judgment against me from which there can be no appeal to a higher court.

Christianity has often been reproached with wallowing in the sinfulness of man, and, in fact, this is often enough a sign of neurotic religiosity. It is a deformation of a property of the biblical relation to God. It points to a fact in the history of religions, that actually the Jewish-

Christian tradition has incredibly intensified the universal consciousness of the judgment that awaits us, in which nothing is forgotten and all is brought to light. "Every careless word that men utter . . ." (Matt. 12:36). "We must all appear before the judgment seat of Christ" (II Cor. 5:10). Why has this happened?

Since within Old Testament prophecy (Second and Third Isaiah) and in the passage from the Old Testament to the New this consciousness grows ever more intense, I know of *only* one answer. The more clearly the covenant of God is known to be a *gracious* covenant, as a covenant of forgiveness, the more acute becomes the consciousness of sin. Therefore in the New Testament, the more radical the divine self-giving and self-sacrifice in Jesus is known to be, and the more it is known in Paul to be intended for *all* men as salvation, the more radical and universal is the language about human sin as the real and deadly danger of man; to this extent Paul is in fact the father of the doctrine of "original sin," which was not to be fully developed until Augustine. And again, as the grace of God in the time of the Reformation was understood once more in a radical and universal sense, the doctrine of original sin was also more sharply formulated. In the case of the Reformers, it could still be conjectured that here for the first time there originated the radical consciousness of sin (or that here for the first time the late-medieval consciousness of sin received more rigorous expression) and that this impelled them to take refuge in grace. But certainly the case is different with Paul; it is from joy in grace, from the indwelling of the Spirit in the soul, that there springs the more rigorous understanding of sin.

In Luther too, at any rate, the *theological* rigor of the doctrine of original sin comes only *after* the new formulation of the doctrines of justification and grace. This means that only when the horizon has been totally *changed* from a horizon *without grace* to a horizon *with grace* that our existence under a horizon without grace, in particular in its aspect of guilt, is seen as one of radical and general despair, of hopelessness and even of horror. Only when freedom has been granted is slavery seen in its complete hideousness; only from the standpoint of joy does one see the complete desperation of the earlier fear; only from the standpoint of the new can one recognize the complete hatefulness of the old. (Karl Barth liked to quote in this context Gustav Schwab's ballad on the Rider over Lake Constance—with one difference indeed, that in the ballad the rider falls dead from his horse in horror at the danger which he has survived, but only now recognized, while for the hearer of the gospel message of salvation, from the horizon of grace, the subsequent knowledge of the total horror of the horizon without grace strengthens his gratitude.)

Thus only as of a danger overcome, in the light of the cross of Christ, are we to speak of the wrath of God, of judgment, and of damnation—and for that very reason not making light of it (on the contrary), but also not speaking with paralyzing effect, nor employing fear as a means to lash people into the knowledge of the necessity of forgiveness and acceptance of it. That is the weakness of the Methodism which follows from Martin Luther's systematization of law and gospel, and which Dietrich Bonhoeffer rightly criticized in his letters from prison. It takes from Christian preaching, as has often happened, the joyfulness of the invitation; it creates anxiety instead of joy, is moralistic and depressing rather than exhilarating.

But this too is connected with the serious, even fatal predicament of our life which the biblical language about God's grace confronts and which it reveals. That is exactly where the biblical witnesses stand; to this they are led by the things they hear and experience—to a perception, without illusions, of a desperate threat. In the light of grace they realize clearly what it means to be without grace.

Philology can help us to get a clearer insight into the Bible's teaching. The German word *Gnade* comes from the Indo-Germanic *neth* (Old Norse *nath*) which is related to *nah* ("near"). It means to incline oneself, to be near, and from that also come the meanings of "help" and "rest." The Irish missionaries used this term, which previously had only a secular significance, to translate *gratia*. The Frankish missionaries preferred the Germanic *huld*: the relationship of the leader to his followers. To the same context of meaning for the translator's task belonged the newly coined Latin word *misericordia*, from which came the German *Barmherzigkeit* ("compassion"). In Greek the place of the heart was taken by the bowels as the place of sympathy, which allows the need of another to touch one "in the inward parts," e.g., Matt. 9:36; 18:27; Luke 7:13; 10:33; 15:20. This behavior, despised by the Greeks, not belonging to the catalog of virtues, not seemly for an aristocrat, for the stoic sage, or for the political Roman, is here valued highly; the word now describes God's ways toward miserable and guilty man.

The Greek *charis* adds, as it were, an aesthetic element. It includes both benevolence and gratitude, and it also includes the beauty that characterizes the Graces. By its assonance with the words *chara* ("joy") and *charma*, which are derived from this root *char-* (that which brings joy—a loving service and charm!), it is an invitation to delight, the delight which a charming, pleasant expression awakens in us; with such delight we look on the face of the gracious God, which moves us to happiness.

That it can be so used shows how right Luther was when he protested against the use of the plural in the scholastic doctrine of grace, occasioned by the different effects of the sacrament (*gratiae*, the sacramental graces), and when he protested against the scholastic distinction between *gratia increata* (the uncreated, incommunicable grace which belongs to God's being) and *gratia creata* (the divine gifts of grace imparted to us in the form of the different *gratiae*). He insisted that grace is singular, it is the favor of God (*favor Dei*) bestowed upon us, God as Person turning to one who can give nothing in return, neither as creature nor (still less) as sinner, and that thus it is identical with God's *agape,* the pure, seeking love of God that asks nothing for itself but everything good for his enemy. Very clearly to be distinguished from this are the *gratiae*, namely the *charismata,* the gifts of God's grace. They are bestowed as the signs of God's favor, but are not identical with it, and this is very important. For from this we can learn that God can be gracious to us, even when he withdraws his gifts from us—and that the visible presence of his gifts does not make the prayer for his favor unnecessary; the giver stands above his gifts.

One can often meet with a certain repugnance on the Jewish side to Christian talk about grace, both because of its apparent limitation to an inward disposition and because of its apparent antithesis between unilateral activity on God's side and complete passivity on man's side. The two Hebrew words *chen* and *chesed,* which Luther—in fact, very incorrectly—translated by "grace" or "compassion," mean not only a disposition but a way of behavior, and indeed not only the behavior of a superior to an inferior but also a reciprocal way of behavior which corresponds to a bond of union which it presupposes. Of this behavior the archaeologist of Israel, Nelson Glueck, in his book about *chesed,* can even say, "It constitutes the true object of a *berith* ("covenant"), and can almost be described as its content." The spectrum of significance embraces covenanted loyalty (Gen. 21:23, King Abimelech to Abraham) and loyal friendship (II Sam. 9:1, 3, 7), and also uncovenanted kindness (Esther 2:9, 17). The most appropriate translation might be "solidarity." According to Nelson Glueck, this is the reason for the making of a covenant, that such behavior should result; this too is the reason for a superior guaranteeing to an inferior the *chesed* of a covenant, in order to make possible for him the behavior of *chesed,* the behavior of true solidarity. "There is," says Glueck, "absolutely no other expression in the Old Testament which . . . represents so exactly the most intimate relation of fellowship between God and his people." In this solidarity stand the Creator and his creation, YHWH and Israel, and it is shown unilaterally by Israel's God even to disloyal Israel; this is the hope of the prophets, this is the hope of Israel on the Yom Kippur (Day of Atonement), and it is fulfilled to the bitter end on Golgotha.

Because of this fact that God's solidarity with us persists even in this one-sidedness, there is in such a connection a bridge from *chesed* to the words "grace" and "compassion," to the Pauline *charis.* The unilateral *chesed*—whether it is that of the Creator, or of the covenant God, or of the forgiving Redeemer—always seeks for reciprocity. Indeed its whole purpose is to seek the reciprocity, the *chesed* answer of the human partner; this is the "true object of the covenant," for it is identical with the good and true life of man.

So the meaning of *chesed* comes close to the Indo-Germanic root of *Gnade* ("grace"): *nahe* ("near"). Grace guarantees reciprocal solidarity, and this annuls my isolation, my despairing self-dependence, my arrogant monadical standing-in-need-of-no-one-else, together with the unbridgeable distance and alienation between I and Thou. The distant Thou becomes the Thou at hand, the distant God becomes the God at hand. Intimate, confident nearness, close intimacy, may come into being where hitherto a horizon without grace was our ultimate environment. Paul called this nearness the "spirit of sonship" through which we cry, "Abba, dear Father!" (Rom. 8:15). The initiative comes, irrevocably, from God, but it brings to man new possibility, a new life-content, solidarity with God as the answer of *gratitude*.

For this there is no equivalent in the other religions, or in philosophical interpretation of the world and of existence. It must have been made very trivial and shallow through long ages of Christian preaching, which forgot joy in its efforts to blacken man, and which forgot mutuality through its emphasis on man's need for consolation and rest,[72] before the men of the Enlightenment rebelled against it. Kant would not hear of justification through grace, and in the same vein Johann Gottfried Seume (1763–1810) wrote in his "Walk to Syracuse": "No good, upright, reasonable man will wish to be saved by grace, not even if a dozen evangelists say so."

At this point it will be worthwhile to speak once more of Karl Marx. In his doctrine of man, through his antireligious animus, and because faith in the creation and the doctrine of grace have often been used to secure human passivity and accommodation of the *status quo*, Marx comes into contradiction with himself. For, just before his polemic against the doctrine of creation (see above), he says very well what he here denies: that my life necessarily has its ground "outside of itself." He says this when he explains that the true, human wealth of man does not consist in things, but in other men; true "human need" is in search of them. *Here*, then, the ideal is not the independence of the solitary man, who has only himself to thank for everything. Rather, the dependence of every man on the rest, and every man's need of his fellowmen, is affirmed as true humanity. But this means that from the start we are dependent on the grace of others, on our gracious neighbor, and the wish to be a Robinson Crusoe standing on one's own feet is a *false* pride. The biblical promise of grace cannot be contradicted by an appeal to such pride; it can only be contradicted by melancholy, by resignation, by the attitude that says: "It would be fine if, over and above the love of human beings for each other, the horizon were not one without grace." It is against this objection, both that of false pride and that which seems to be based on resignation, that the promise of grace is directed.

However, the promise of grace does not aim at passivity but, on the contrary, at activity. Passive reception occurs where something falls into my lap, not only without my cooperation but also without the cooperation of another. But if the gift comes from a giving, from the action of another, it creates an interpersonal relationship in which I cannot remain passive. For if I remained passive, I would have remained unaware that it was not chance, not fate, not nature, but this other person that has done an action upon me with the gift. This turning to me of the other person is lost, it is dissipated, if I refuse to accept the gift, or if I accept it without response, without on my side taking up the relation created by the agent.

Grace is more than the gift which it gives; it is the turning to me of the giver himself. When Marx says in the passage quoted above that "the self-sufficiency of nature and of man is inconceivable" because "it contradicts all the visible evidence of practical life," he concedes, against his own will, a certain truth to the impression that I am not a self-subsistent being. No one owes to himself the fact that he is there. On the contrary, our begetting and our birth are an extremely dictatorial interference with us, a most blatant contradiction of our autonomy. Without our being asked, we are condemned to existence.

But is there not also a truth in Marx's objection? He

raises it in a very one-sided manner in resentment against the talk of creation and grace that opposes our freedom. At the end of the preface to his doctoral dissertation (1841), in opposition to all faith in God, he proclaims the confession of Prometheus, "In one word, I hate all gods," as the confession of philosophy "so long as a single drop of blood pulses in its world-compelling absolutely free heart." This, says Marx, is "its own verdict against all heavenly and earthly gods, which do not acknowledge human self-consciousness as the highest divinity. There shall be no other alongside of him. . . . Prometheus is the most notable martyr and saint in the philosophical calendar."[73]

The antithesis to Christian faith seems insuperable. By both sides, by the Christians and then by the Marxists, this opposition has been set up as insuperable, from secret political motives, and it is just this which obliges theological thought to call it into question.

It is life that is under consideration. It is dictated to us: that is the one truth which is obvious to us. But life, and especially human, conscious life, is at the same time *eo ipso* activity. That is what Marx has in mind. Here passive reception is identical with becoming active. Life only becomes life when it is being lived. So completely does the gift of life aim at our activity that it is lost when we refuse to live it, and we live it by the very act of breathing. So passive are we in relation to this gift that it is nearly unthinkable that we might be able to refuse it when it is given to us. The infant at any rate cannot refuse; he fulfills by compulsion the free act of breathing. Even the suicide called back to life by artificial respiration cannot refuse to breathe. So powerful is life in us that even the rescued suicide can only attempt afresh, by other artificial means, to bring to an end once more this powerful life, the freedom to live. Life is at one and the same time (against Marx) the gift that is received by us in passivity, whose ground lies irrevocably beyond us, *and* (with Marx) at the same time our own activity, our own action; with every breath we breathe we are ourselves the creators of our life. This is what the word of grace means in the biblical sense—and this is true even of the grace of creation; in every moment we are both completely receptive and completely active. What we have here discussed in conversation with Marx is only a repetition of the most debated question of the doctrine of grace in Christian theology: Grace is either merely an offer, and only becomes a reality when with our freedom we grasp the offered hand (this is the teaching of Pelagianism and semi-Pelagianism, including Erasmus and many pietists); or it is *gratia irresistibilis*, "irresistible grace" (in the consistent expressions of Reformation theology, as in Luther's *De servo arbitrio*, where he cites the process of birth; and in the Calvinistic doctrine of predestination).

For Karl Barth the assertion of both positions together is central. Barth speaks of grace as a reality (not a mere possibility!) which comes from God alone, and for that very reason he speaks of human freedom. How is this to be understood?

Here help is to be found in the central concept that Barth uses in this context with mediating force: *gratitude*. Gratitude is an event in human life that is analogous to the "dialectical" unity of passivity and activity in physical life, especially when we are considering the *essential* character of the event of gratitude. An example of unessential, i.e., accidental, gratitude, not constitutive of a relationship between human beings, is the expression "Thank you" which we use out of wholly laudable politeness for a gift, which perhaps is not even freely given, but as a duty, or in exchange in return for our money, e.g., a railway ticket at the booking office. The *essence* of gratitude is that we answer gratefully: (*a*) not

only to a gift but to an act of giving; (*b*) where in the gift
the giving of the other as such expresses itself as a gift of
his approach to us, as the gift of his *person*, his friendship, his love, his existence for me; (*c*) where this giving
is a *free* act, not a compelled, automatic, reflex action, but
human and personal in character.

Even if we can accept the gift itself as such without
thanking for it, simply snatching it and using it, yet we
can only accept this free personal existence for us—the
true gift in the material gift—in gratitude, in an answering approach toward the giver. His approach to us is
more than a material gift, it is the giving of life, and here
the dialectic we spoke of holds good: here we are at the
same time wholly passive and wholly active, wholly
dependent (irreversibly so) and wholly active. But the
latter can be so only *because* of the former. By approach-
ing us the giver calls forth our gratitude; we owe our
gratitude not to ourselves, but wholly to him. We are not
previously *free* to thank him, but we only *become* free to
thank him through his approach to us. Our freedom is not
the freedom of choice—whether we should thank him or
not—but the irresistible answer spontaneously breaking
forth, the freedom to thank him which has been bestowed upon us. We would have to suppress this artificially, and to oppose it, and doing so would certainly not
be an expression of our freedom, but of our bondage, our
incapacity for gratitude, our stony coldness under the
sunlight of this approach.

Gratitude is the *natural* thing under this sunlight, the
natural consummation of new life; to withhold it—to
prefer our bondage—would be the choice of suicide, a
deliberate regression into the old life. The analogy with
the gift of physical life here admittedly breaks down. For
this is the place where *decision* comes in, as to whether
we are to allow this natural process to run its course, to
breathe in the new life, or whether we are deliberately to

struggle back into the old life of lack of fellowship, of isolation from others, of being-turned-in-upon-oneself (Luther), and are to adhere to this old life artificially.

The Heidelberg Catechism placed the exposition of the Decalogue at the end, after describing the gracious approach of God in Jesus Christ to our existence, lost in the old life. It placed the Ten Commandments under the rubric "Of Gratitude." This is better than the arrangement chosen by Luther in his Catechisms. There the law of God is only a stern demand by which we are measured, before which we are found wanting—a demand which becomes an accusation and a judgment upon us and consequently an expression of the horizon without grace, from which the *gospel* sets us free. For Luther this was a consequence of the Pauline polemic against the *nomos* ("law"), but this is exegetically inaccurate and doctrinally unsound. Barth speaks more correctly of the sequence "gospel and law," for *Torah* is not "law" but the guidance for life given on the basis of the covenant, guidance to free, grateful life under the promise of the presence of the covenant God for his covenant partners. The exhortations of the apostolic letters are to be understood in the same sense, as can be clearly seen from Rom. 12:1–4.

Christian ethics is the question: What do we see when we look at our life in concrete detail as gratitude for "the immeasurable riches of his grace" (Eph. 2:7)? What do we see when the following things are clear: (*a*) Gratitude as a life lived in relation to the giver always means not mere feeling and sentiment but a *life* lived, i.e., an action as well as a sentiment. (*b*) This action is accomplished in harmony of disposition with that of the giver, which awakens me to gratitude, that is, in love (*agape*). (*c*) The living of this life means a concern for the interests of the giver, and cooperation with his interests. Here then, surely, the life of gratitude means an interest in the saving work of the giver, which reached out to us, and in which work we are now invited to share. This must be depicted in the life of the person who is grateful for it, in a human world characterized by the struggle for life.

RECOMMENDED READING

Iwand, Hans Joachim. *Gesetz und Evangelium*. Nachgelassene Werke, Vol. 40. 1964.
Klappert, Bertold. *Promissio und Bund. Gesetz und Evangelium bei Luther und Barth*. 1976.
Kreck, Walter. *Grundfragen christlicher Ethik*. 1975.
Pannenberg, Wolfhart. *Gottesgedanke und menschliche Freiheit*. 1972. (E. T., see *The Idea of God and Human Freedom*. Westminster Press, 1973.)

X   Discipleship in the Conflicts of the World

Forgiveness is new mission to the world. But this world is a world of conflicting ideas and interests. The disciples of Jesus must not withdraw from the responsibility of cooperating in their ordering, under their conditions. In doing so, however, they will be involved in these conflicts. Here the main problem is that of political power. How can this work well? How is this to be reconciled with their new life?

"Grace must find expression in life, otherwise it is not grace." So runs a decisive thesis of Karl Barth,[74] which, after what we have said, will be intelligible, even natural, not to say tautological. For if grace is bestowal of life, then it creates life, and life is activity in every second; so its purpose is activity and not passivity. To remain passive would then be equivalent to a failure to receive grace, a refusal to receive it, or, more exactly, the failure to take advantage of and put into action the life possibilities given to us with the reality of the grace that comes to us.

Through their opposition to God, and their lives lived in enmity to God, people bring death upon themselves, and the death sentence of divine judgment. If God's gracious saving approach gives such persons acquittal from this death sentence,[75] then this important concept of acquittal at once requires amplification. It could be misunderstood in analogy to the judgment of a human court, as if the acquitted persons, without anything more being done, were now left to continue their old lives, in which the old corruption could only repeat itself.

So then Luther adds at once to the acquittal what the

divine acquittal, in contrast with that of a human court, inseparably contains and brings with it: "Where there is forgiveness of sins, there is also life and blessedness."[76] We have defined "blessedness" as delight in seeing the face of the gracious God. But it is quite impossible to understand the significance of "life" intensively and extensively enough. "Grace is the taking possession of the whole of existence," says Christoph Blumhardt. The acquittal is at the same time an appointment, namely, an appointment to be a co-worker with God, *cooperator Dei in mundo,* to collaborate, not in our liberation, our acquittal (for this would bring us back to semi-Pelagianism, and the counting of percentages!), but in the world, in God's creation, previously ruined by us. If this perhaps was the concern of the Catholic tradition's assertion, in opposition to the Reformers, about man's cooperation (though it was then expressed in a very misleading way), then it must (with correction of the mistake) be positively accepted. Cooperation is then, as Hans Küng writes,[77] not a working alongside God, but a "sharing in the activity that God alone set in motion"—both a participation in the new life given to us through realization of its new possibilities and also a sharing in God's great work of salvation in the world of men. "For everything which does not lose through being imparted to others [and grace is a case in point], one does not possess as one should without giving it to others."[78] Precisely this is the connection between the gracious love of God and the commandment to love, between the love toward God which answers the love of God and the other love, which is "like unto it" (Matt. 22:39), i.e., love directed toward our fellowmen. Only the two taken together are the life bestowed and willed by grace, the *one* answer of gratitude.

I cannot love God without devoting my whole heart in living for the sake of my fellowmen, without

devoting my entire soul in response to all the spiritual trends in the world around me, without devoting
all my strength to this God in his correlation with
man.[79]

Acquittal is being designated, empowered, and
equipped for cooperation in God's work. That is the
content of the New Testament word *pneuma* ("Spirit"),
in which the indicative and the imperative—the indicative of the real liberation which comes from God and
from him alone, and the imperative to fulfill that life of
grace which "wills to be lived"—are indissolubly bound
together. "If we live by the Spirit, let us also walk by the
Spirit!" (Gal. 5:25).

Life is freedom, and freedom is power. One who is
called from nothing into being (Rom. 4:17) can do what
before he could not do: breathe and act. One who is
raised from the dead can do what as a dead man he could
no longer do: breathe and act. What before was impossible now becomes possible. Not one of the biblical
challenges, which we are accustomed to call "commandments," tells us of anything which would have been
effortlessly possible for us without a fundamental liberation and a new equipment of the Spirit. How should the
unshakable trust in God of which we have spoken be
possible without an approach of God, which calls it forth
afresh? And how should the fulfillment of the First
Commandment be possible for us, the risk of refusing
obedience and worship to all the powers which set
themselves up as the gods of our life? How should it be
possible for us to fulfill the commandment "Thou shalt
not kill," both literally in a world in which daily in
manifold ways we are drawn to participate in killing and
also in the radicalized sense in which Jesus expounds it
in the Sermon on the Mount (Matt. 5:21), which refers
back to the fundamental will of God? How should it be

possible for us not only at the best to tolerate our
fellowman, not only not to do to him what we would not
wish to be done to us, but to do to him that which we
wish to be done to us? (Matt. 7:12.) In the teaching of
Jesus the so-called Golden Rule is positively formulated,
not negatively, as in Confucius. How then should love be
possible for us as we are, love which deserves to be
called existence for others?

The commandments are the descriptions of the new
possibilities that are opened up to us through "Immanuel," through the presence with us of the God of grace.
They too must be believed. We cannot first ascertain that
we have them, and then put them into action. Rather, we
must rely on the fact that he who here challenges us also
gives us the freedom to act, and therefore—in view of his
possibilities, in which we must put our faith—we must
do what he says, things that we do not see ourselves
capable of doing when we look at our visible possibilities. Kant's maxim "You can because you ought" is thus
not wholly wrong. But if the commandments are to be
understood as commandments of grace, the formula must
be changed: "You ought, then you can." The disciples of
Jesus are called to achieve the impossible. Therefore
they take up the impossible existence of sheep among
wolves (Matt. 10:16). They proclaim as God's will a good
life which, under the conditions of this real world of ours,
appears impossible—and if so, "so much the worse for
the reality."

Just at this point what was said in Chapter VIII about
the present and future character of the Kingdom of God
becomes important. If the Kingdom of God were only in
the future, then it would bring to an end this world of
time, and could only stand in a negative relation to it. But
as a future penetrating the present, it must be thought of
as an already operating factor, and this cannot then be an
abstract and general negation. God's new reality, which

in contrast with the old dominion of death we called "the Kingdom of God," does not mean a life of angels and the blessed dead in the hereafter. It means the change of our present life from the movement toward death to the movement toward life, and this change is made, not in total negation of the environment and the previous way of life, but in selective affirmation and rejection, in change of priorities, in forsaking old alliances and entry into new alliances, etc.

This is true not only for the history of the individual but also for the history of the world. The changed life of the disciples of Jesus penetrates into society in the form of ideas, moral evaluations, and questionings and here forms alliances with other traditions, also with changing interests. Whether defense or criticism of the existing order at this or that time follows from the gospel will often enough be a matter of debate within the disciple fellowship itself, and this argument within the church is also of interest to those outside it, because it is an argument between members of society, and because ideas and interests are involved in its positions which also have relevance and advocates outside the church.

The responsibility for this influence upon world history and on the whole of society must not be disclaimed by the disciple circle. Today, two thousand years after primitive Christianity, it consists not only in shared guilt and remorse but also in initiatives whereby the attack of the gospel is brought to bear upon the social aspects of sin, the inhumanities of contemporary society. Thus we draw our conclusions today from the profoundly contradictory picture presented by the history of Christianity, more contradictory than any other culture known to us. It is the history of ever-renewed impulses and thrusts for the humanizing of society—and at the same time it is the history of ever-renewed horrors, those which rage within the peoples of Christendom (e.g., Inquisition, witch-hunting), and others which have been brought upon the peoples of the other continents, culminating at last in the barbarism of our century. The new powers seem to be disavowed by this history, but of itself it forces us to seek for the original dynamic, the explosion in which this history took its rise. It kindled so great a hope; it was not merely the upsurge of new ideas, but of new certainties and possibilities of life, and it was never wholly blocked and stifled by what people made of it. Time after time there were new explosions. We ask now concerning the life of the persons who were seized and transformed by this explosion in the midst of the unchanged, unrenewed world, and in asking this we make one premise, and have one definite assurance. The *premise* is that the disavowal of the new life—because of its defeats and the victories of the old life even in, and especially in, the history of Christianity—has not annihilated that explosion. There are (or, speaking from a Christian standpoint, *he* gives us) even today disciples and a community of disciples who follow him, however scattered they may be in the world, "Abrahamic communities," as Dom Helder Câmara calls them. The *assurance* is that the time of the reality, i.e., the effectiveness of that explosion, does not lie behind us, but is still and always before us.

We shall now look at the environment of the central event, Jesus Christ, the attack of the new life upon the old. We look at the *ecclesia*. We look both at the individual and at the fellowship into which the individual, reached and apprehended by the invitation to cooperate, is at once incorporated (Baptism) because the new life, as a human life, is at the same time a social life (Communion):

a. I cannot live it alone, because it must take the form of a fellowship, as a new social life.

b. I cannot live it alone, because I need the help and the correction of the others.

c. I ought not to live it alone, because the others need me.

d. Together we ought to live it with each other in the midst of the rest, for their sake, as salt, light, leaven for their social life.

The designation "Christian" is not the concept of an ideal. Otherwise who could say, "I am a Christian"? I am a Christian, not as a visible saint, but as *simul justus et peccator* ("at the same time a righteous person and a sinner"), as a battlefield between the new and the old.

Thus "Christian" is not a concept of religious statistics, distinguishing one world view from others and implying that I alone have the truth, that elsewhere there is darkness. Rather, I leave open the question of how far God's Spirit also works for new life outside the church. I myself have heard this explicit call through the message, and can orientate myself by it. That binds me with the others, who are in the same situation, into a common life. I am thus bound, not against the others who do not hear it, or do not listen to it, or reject it, but in their favor and for them. Insofar as it is a "privilege" to hear this explicit call, I have this privilege *for* the others, not that I may exalt myself, but in order to serve them with it. (This is the meaning of *every* privilege from the standpoint of the new life. The new life does not make me equal in possession, but only equal in service.) My privilege is the standard by which I am more strictly judged than the others. "Every one to whom much is given, of him will much be required, and of him to whom men commit much they will demand the more" (Luke 12:48).

"Christian" is thus a title which means fellowship grace given, pardon, and commission (mission).

Becoming a Christian is a change in this world, of life in this world, not a removal into another, transcendent life. It is indeed a being summoned out of my previous life, but a being summoned into my previous world, into the world of the old life. From this it follows that I come into contradiction (*a*) with myself as a product of the old world (= battlefield), and (*b*) with my environment. This latter contradiction is now our theme.

This contradiction is *radical* but not *total*. The anchorites and monks thought of it as total. This was not simply wrong. It *can* serve the mission of the whole group (= *ecclesia*) when parts of it know themselves called to exemplify the *radical* nature of the contradiction by a *total* withdrawal from society. But this can never have more than exceptional, compensatory significance, underlining the indisputable mission of the community into the old world, for the old world.

1. That the contradiction is not *total* is shown by the fact that mission clearly implies living with those to whom one is sent, living *their* life with them, speaking their language, sharing in their life problems, speaking to them, not from outside, but as one of their own people.

2. This also implies that not *everything* in the old life is wrong. What is wrong in the old life comes from its contradiction to the life of a created being, which it still always is at the same time; i.e., it is still a life willed and affirmed by God, daily equipped in many bodily and spiritual ways. I share in this, and take part in it, in the natural basis, the work for maintenance of life, in intellectual life with its knowledge and innovations, in joy, pleasure, and grief, in the whole range of man's divinely given powers. A too-pious renunciation of cultural life is a sin against faith in the Creator.

3. For this reason there is not a total renunciation of the morality of the old life. Human morality is indeed, as Marxists often forget, not simply a class product. However deeply it is stamped by the class society and exploited for the purposes of class domination, it contains a plus over and above the existing order, an inkling of the good life, an element of criticism directed against things as

they are—especially where, however much accommodated to the existing order, it is (as in our cultural milieu) a deposit of the influence of Christian preaching. For this reason primitive Christianity takes up the theme of ancient morality: "Whatever is honorable, whatever is just, whatever is pure, whatever is lovely, whatever is gracious, if there is any excellence, if there is anything worthy of praise, think about these things" (Phil. 4:8). But it does this of course not indiscriminately, but selecting critically.

However, this selection implies an acknowledgment that the world around us is not simply forsaken by God, not wholly opposed to God, but preserved by God by means of insights and guidelines for the direction of life which are good and true, which even we ambassadors of the new life have to acknowledge, to tend and foster, and to learn. This in itself is the basis of a relation of dialogue; it causes these ambassadors to be not only instructors and critics but also hearers and learners, and this especially where (e.g., as missionaries) they go into another cultural sphere. The word of Paul could have protected them from unreflectingly propagating the maxims of their cultural sphere of the West (perhaps because of a Christian veneer) as maxims of the Kingdom of God, and for that reason having a destructive influence on the culture that they find before them. Karl Barth says, very finely:

> How does Christian ethics relate itself to the world of human morality; that is, to the manners and customs, to the old, and also to the new, to the traditional or perhaps revolutionary life-principles, in which man thinks that, in apparent independence of that history, he can know and do "the good"? To this we must answer: Christian ethics goes through this whole world of morality, tries all things, and holds to the best, only the best, and that means just

whatever at any time praises God's grace the best. It cannot but be that the Christian ethic will continually provide new surprises for man with his moral standards.[80]

Barth's word "surprises" is admittedly a mild word for the radical nature of the contradiction. This becomes evident when we make clear to ourselves that the contradiction is not so much directed against the productions of our spirit (morals) as against those of our "heart" and their precipitate in the social order, against us ourselves, as stamped by this world, which we continually stamp even more deeply by what we are.

This world is *Cain's world*. We are Cain. That is what the Yahwist writer says in Genesis 4. But it is the world of Cain which—rather than perishing from its Cain nature—is to be saved, transformed, and, with a view to this salvation, *maintained*. This is part of the divine work in which the new group is to share, the preservation of the old world with a view to its salvation.

We will unfold the whole difficulty of the matter set forth in this proposition:

1. As we have seen, it is not possible for us to remove ourselves as the new men from the old world, to emphasize our otherness clearly in isolation, as an isolated island. This is a natural tendency and it happened as early as the days of primitive Christianity (cf. II Cor. 6:14–18, probably an un-Pauline gloss). As we have already said, withdrawal, the separation of individuals, is not excluded. But this must never be an example for the fellowship, but only a spiritual reinforcement for its entry into the world, whose difficulty is: not to separate, but also not to conform (Rom. 12:2). Not to be separated, but still to be different, other than the world! How will that happen?

2. They themselves are not totally different, not totally

new, but a battlefield. It would therefore be very necessary for them to separate themselves, without further contamination by the old, in order to rid themselves wholly, in a protected environment, of the relics of the old life that still adhere to them, without being exposed, as men still liable to infection, to the continuing danger of contagion through daily contact with the old life. They are still themselves not yet "converted," mature and stable enough for this mission as "sheep among wolves" (Matt. 10:16), for their wolf nature is by no means yet adequately expelled. Will they not—still wolves in sheep's clothing—soon howl again with the wolves? What will happen?

3. The old world (as it seems) by no means requires the cooperation of Christians in order to preserve itself. It is indeed already busily engaged in the task of self-preservation; indeed, self-preservation is its highest principle, and for this purpose it has always used institutions and methods with all its ingenuity to preserve men *from each other* as well as in community *with each other*. If we are speaking of Cain's world, then we think first of all of men's preservation from each other; man is man's greatest enemy. Potentially every one of us would put another to the sword in order to save his own life. The cruelty of history does not consist in the great catastrophes of nature, but in the motives of man's life, as Brecht's *Threepenny Opera* says:

> For what does man live by?
> By hourly torturing, fleecing, attacking,
>   strangling, and devouring;
> Only by this does man live, that he so
>   completely
> Can forget that he is a man
> My friends, make no bones about it,
> Man lives by nothing but his crimes![81]

That is the truth in the statement in *The Communist Manifesto*, "The history of all society in the past is the

history of class struggles."[82] Whether possession and
pleasure or security or naked survival is given as the true
goal, it is always the tough will to survive that impels
individuals and collectives against one another in order
to secure their own lives at any price and at the cost of
others. We can now describe the task of Christians in
preserving the world according to God's will thus: they
must play their part in ensuring that this murderous
conflict does not wholly destroy the world of Cain, but,
rather, that men may see that togetherness is a better way
of preservation than conflict, and that practical consequences are drawn from this insight. Thus the practical
task of Christians has often and correctly been described.
But this does not bring into sufficiently sharp focus the
difficulty which they encounter in this part of their task
of mission.

This insight is not one contributed by the Christians
alone; it is already common knowledge. That self-preservation against one another could end with universal
annihilation is known also by the wisdom of the old
world. For this reason, limits are repeatedly set to the
struggle for self-preservation against each other: within
the social collective by law, custom, and morality, whereby the weaker receives his fundamental rights and is not
destroyed by the mailed fist of the stronger; and between
the collectives by a law regulating the relations of collectives. The latter—international law—was always less
developed than law within the collective, and to this day
is without effective sanctions and sufficiently powerful
courts to enforce it. But there have never been wanting
attempts—by means of all kinds of mutual agreements,
treaties, and so on—to protect nations from universal
destruction, even when these, e.g., in the contemporary
atom bomb pact, are limited to mutual assurances that
the other side also wishes to avoid the risk of a major
atomic war.

Here too those commissioned to collaborate in the

preservation of human beings will plead—as allies of the already existing wisdom—for the further development of hitherto feeble initiatives to replace international jungle law by binding international law with authoritative and influential courts. Everywhere they will be advocates of togetherness rather than conflict. The question is only this: Since here they take part as allies in already existing activities for self-preservation which are motivated by the self-interest of the others, will their cooperation only amount to being taken in tow by those who from self-interest have thought out methods of common self-preservation, methods that merely bring conflicting interests within a framework that secures the preservation of all, without removing the conflict? *Or* will they press on beyond that point to measures which not only prevent the conflict from running to its logical conclusion of mutual annihilation or the victory of the stronger, but which also assail it as itself an evil state of affairs, and one that deforms men?

4. There is another difficulty. All historical life in community, i.e., the limitation of conflict by means of legal institutions which make possible a minimum of togetherness, works with the same weapon that men use to assert their will against each other and to obtain their livelihood and subsistence at the cost of others, with *coercion*. Coercion is the fundamental structure of all society, all communal life in historical time (with the solitary exception of some prehistoric societies, including pygmies, bushmen, etc., today). Certainly there are other ways of getting security for one's life, e.g., intelligence. But what such means earn, without coercion, is *preserved* by coercion. This is the fundamental means for preserving *inequality* in property, in life possibilities, in security, in development of personality, and in enjoyment. Togetherness, the possibility of Cain men living together, is preserved through coercion, through law

within the collective, with the threat of sanctions. But
this law with its coercion simultaneously preserves the
conflict, the unequal life of some at the cost of others.
Indeed the preservation of togetherness has as its goal
the preservation of the conflict through prevention of the
danger bound up with this conflict, the mutual war of all
against all.

This is the mode of preservation which those who are
commissioned to collaborate with God's will for preservation find confronting them. Now it becomes clear that
the preservation of the world—as a counteractive to the
destructive consequences of conflict and in favor of a
togetherness which gives security to life—is already in
progress through the insight of human reason, before
those awakened to cooperate in God's work come on the
scene. God is already at work in the world that forsakes
him but is not forsaken by him—through human reason.
That was expounded in the theological tradition in the
doctrine of the *conservatio mundi* ("preservation of the
world") as an action of God external to the gospel and
faith; and thereby reason, the state, law, and even coercion in the service of law were affirmed to be the gift of
God.

For those commissioned by the new life, for the
disciples of Jesus, this gives rise to a difficulty. It appears
that in the world of Cain, in the world of wolves, in the
world of those who will to assert themselves against each
other, a togetherness is possible which at least to some
extent prevents their mutual destruction—above all, the
destruction of the weaker by the stronger—and which
compels the wolves to mutual tolerance and support.
Such togetherness is apparently a condition of *law*—not
to be asserted and maintained except by the application
of coercion. If these observations are true, how can
disciples of Jesus, who have Jesus' Sermon on the Mount
ringing in their ears, with its repudiation of coercion as a

description of the new life, participate in the maintenance of law by coercion?

5. And now there comes a further difficulty. In order to exercise coercion, *power* is needed. In order to use coercion against the coercion of conflict in order to maintain togetherness—i.e., in order to use legal coercion, coercion in the service of justice, for the enforcement of laws—power in the state is needed. But power in the state is always the product of political struggles. Political struggles are always struggles about power in the state, about the possession of that position from which the laws, the concrete regulations of togetherness, are enunciated—that position which controls the means of coercion for the execution of these regulations. Every political constellation of power is the result of such struggles and must continually defend itself against the efforts of others to come to power and change the existing regulations. It must consequently fight to maintain itself, and must set in motion the means of coercion at its disposal both to enforce the laws for the communal life passed by it and in order to fight for its own existence.

The subjects in these struggles for the power of the state are almost always groups in society for which—within the context of the hitherto existing class societies—the issue at stake is the maintenance of their material privileges won in the conflict, or the winning of such privileges. If a group united not by such privileges but by ideology gains power in the state, it has then swiftly attached to itself the interest of privilege, and amalgamated it with the ideological interest, as, e.g., in the history of Islam or of the Puritan revolution, or in Soviet communism. In the French Revolution the egalitarian ideas were from the outset a mere facade for the interests of the bourgeois class, just as they are where Christian ideas legitimate the seizure of power (e.g., when the German princes and towns went over to Protestantism). This does not mean the denial of the active power of ideas and the innovations caused by them; however, this native power is not great enough by itself to carry the day, and not powerful enough to prevent it from becoming subservient to other interests.

The difficulty is that those who are called to cooperate with God's work in the maintenance of the world can only do so if they participate in the political struggle for power.

a. But here—when the interests of privilege, ideologically disguised, are everywhere at work, and when those who are called share in these interests themselves—what will happen? What will prevail in me: the challenge to commit myself to a togetherness in which the conflict is transcended, or my material interest, which wishes for only such a regulation of togetherness as does not infringe my possession of privileges which have been won in the conflict?

b. And can I, the more I have become a disciple of Jesus, take part at all in political struggles? Do these not necessarily imply the treatment of other people as enemies, which is impossible for me? Does not one need for this a strong will to power over other men, and does not the disciple of Jesus lose more and more the taste and practical skill for this? Is political struggle possible without alliances with men and groups whose only aim is to assert their own interests, with "old" men, i.e., with men in whom the old nature still reigns unchallenged, and will it not be more probable that I, the disciple in this alliance, will become *their* tool instead of their becoming mine? Is political struggle thinkable without the methods of intrigue, of deceit, of demagoguery, not to mention worse methods—methods which must be deeply repugnant, even impossible, to the disciple of Jesus?

So the opinion is very understandable that politics, "the dirty business," cannot be a field in which disciples can cooperate in the maintenance of the world. There are other spheres and ways for this operation of theirs, personal life with its influence on the environment, professional activity, education, medicine, art, and especially Christian witness to men's hearts. Do not the shining examples of Christian character seem to be incapable of politics: a Francis of Assisi, Dostoevsky's Alyosha in *The Brothers Karamazov?* *Indirect* influence on the shaping of world affairs seems to us to have more promising and adequate Christian prospects, to be more in agreement with Christian identity, than direct participation. As a great example we must mention the Quakers.

But this last sentence already implies that *non*participation, absolute lack of interest, does not come into the question. Where that is proclaimed as Christian, God is refused participation in his work of preservation, and an area so important as the shaping of society is withdrawn from God's saving attack. It is an indispensable part of the task of the disciple in this world that he should accompany political events attentively, prayerfully, sharing in reflection and in consultation, now and then giving his judgment and taking sides. This, to take an example, is the way of the Quakers.

But this limitation to indirect participation cannot be satisfactory, and therefore it cannot be a limitation as a matter of principle, but only one based on personal vocation and endowment, or imposed by outward circumstances. The belief that in such indirect participation we are wholly excluded from direct participation is an illusion. Our activity in our profession connects us with politics and confronts us continually with political decisions, e.g., entry into a trade union or employers' association. It is for my advantage that the interest groups to which I belong are fighting, whether I like it or not, and one of them is my state in its national competitive struggle with other states, e.g., as a colonial and imperialist power, in its wars into which I am drawn, and which I support in any case by my professional activity, and as a member of a people under mobilization. I am a taxpayer in parliamentary states a citizen with a vote, and not even refusal to vote or refusal of military service can release me from participating in the common destiny, i.e., the profits, conflicts, and misfortunes of my state.

And this cannot release me from the responsibility which must then be exercised in *direct* participation, because the shaping of public affairs, especially legislation and foreign policy, must not be left in the hands of those who are not disturbed by the attack of God—and thus not in the least even beginning to repent—and who are following *only* their own interests or ideas that have not submitted to the critique of the gospel. We may twist and turn as we like; we are already involved in politics, and therefore we must go into politics; we have not the choice of taking part in politics or not, but only of *how* to take part, with what motives, with what aims and methods, on which side. Here, then, we shall have a decisive confirmatory test, which we must not evade, though it may prove divisive.

In the following pages I choose as a special question not the often-debated question of coercion, but the question concerning the significance and effect of laws. Laws are the regulations passed by the possessors of state power, whether democratically delegated and controlled or not, regulations for the intercourse of society, together with coercive sanction for their implementation. But *togetherness* is the goal to which the interest of disciples attaches itself. At this point, as we have seen, the divine and the human endeavors for preservation coincide; the conflict in the will to self-preservation endangers preservation, the togetherness has the success of preservation as its consequence. In togetherness also coincide the needs of the present and the aim of God's activity, the Kingdom of God. That is preservation here and now, and the goal at which preservation aims. For life in the Kingdom of God is perfect togetherness without any conflict, "peace and joy in the Holy Spirit" (Rom. 14:17), the kingdom of brotherhood in which swords are turned into plowshares and spears into pruning hooks, and in which "they shall sit every man under his vine and his fig tree, and none shall make them afraid" (Micah 4:3f.), and "one man shall invite another under his vine and under his fig tree" (Zech. 3:10).

Thus participation in the political arena is enjoined on disciples, with the *aim* of supporting those efforts to increase togetherness as far as is possible under the conditions of the old world; and this aim is at the same time the *criterion* by which tendencies, theories, attitudes, and alliances of the disciples are measured.

This is a different criterion from that which was often given in theological tradition. There what was proposed was often the acceptance of an immutable *order,* described either as an order of creation, or as an order of preservation, consisting of a number of ordinances (marriage, the family, the state), which were statically defined in terms of essence. This meant that Christians were automatically forced onto the conservative side.[83] In contrast, our definition is a *dynamic* criterion which aims at the reduction of conflict and is consequently critical of the minimal goal of a togetherness which can only give stability to the hierarchy of privileges resulting from conflict, and which continually presses on beyond this toward more togetherness, more equality, more solidarity, and toward a life lived less at the cost of others, aiming continually at a life in common, by means of agencies and achievement organized in common.

RECOMMENDED READING

Burgsmüller, Alfred (ed.). *Zum politischen Auftrag der christlichen Gemeinde* (Barmen II). *Votum des Theo-*

logischen Ausschusses der Evangelischen Kirche der Union. 1974.

Dannemann, Ulrich. *Theologie und Politik im Denken Karl Barths.* 1977.

Girardi, Giulio. *Marxismus und Christentum.* 1968.

Metz, Johann Baptist. *Glaube in Geschichte und Gesellschaft. Studien zu einer praktischen Fundamentaltheologie.* 1977.

XI Justice and Peace as a Task of the Disciple Community in the Conflicts of This World: On the Fifth Thesis of the Barmen Declaration*

The community of Jesus' disciples commits itself, under the conditions of the present "old" world, to readjustments of the law that will distribute "to each man his due." It also advocates the right of every individual to use his freedom within the bounds of the community. The ideal of corporate responsibility and cooperation of all leads to critical questions addressed to the contemporary social order, and to advocacy of a better, socialist order.

"Under the conditions of the old aeon," that is, under the conditions of guilt and death, we are concerned about the togetherness of those who are still "old" men, men who strive against each other, ruthlessly exploit each other, deliberately assert themselves at the expense of others. Two things can be said:

1. This implies *eschatological reserve*. The motive of Christian commitment is indeed love, and its goal is a togetherness such as will be fully realized in the King-

---

*TRANSLATOR'S NOTE: The Barmen Declaration. In May 1934, the German "Confessing Church," formed by those who were alarmed at the threat of National Socialism and of the so-called "German Christians" to the freedom of the church and the gospel over against the state, met at Barmen and issued six theses denouncing the "German Christian" claims as heretical. For a full account, see *Evangelisches Kirchen-Lexicon* (Vandenhoeck & Ruprecht), Paragraphs 309–313.

dom of God. But every condition thinkable on earth will still be stamped by sin and death; it cannot be an approximation, but at the best is a parable of the Kingdom of God.[84]

2. Hence, even the means will be determined by the fact that we are concerned with the greatest degree of togetherness for us, who are still "old" men, who have to a large degree to be compelled to come together by coercion which opposes our use of coercion in order to obtain advantages over each other, and by laws which are associated with coercion. For this reason disciples must not hold themselves aloof from the political struggle concerning legislation and the power to legislate.

We will concentrate for the moment on the question of shared responsibility and the cooperation of Christians for the regulation of human life in community by means of laws. When we speak of laws here we mean both the codified laws in the narrower sense of the word, issued by the state and conjoined with the threat of sanctions; and also their cultural presuppositions, the customs, morality, and general systems of value ("basic values") and disciplines for the regulation of instinct.

Thus it is clear that the Christian goal here is not the setting up of the Kingdom of God; it is not an ordering of life that presupposes renewed men and hearts. The goal is, rather, the preservation and improvement of the community life of sinners, of men with the stamp of Cain. Here too cooperation for this goal occurs under the directive of God's Lordship; here too we are concerned with the realization of God's will, which not only relates to "those who are his," to the reborn, but is his gracious will for all men, even for those who are living in opposition to him.

This declaration of the goal sounds conservative. Without our noticing, it could turn into preservation of the *status quo*. This would then only be a codification of the advantages, privileges, and inequality which have been established in the mutual conflict in the past; it would thus be a glorification of injustice as justice.

If God's command of preservation is not to be ideologically misused to sanctify the *status quo* in this manner, then the interposition of Christians in the regulation of togetherness must always have a critical character, with a view to *better law*. There must be an affirmation of law, and at the same time a critical realization that the present law still *also* serves to preserve injustice. In this sense we must understand Martin Luther's fine saying about the blessing of human law; he praises not the actual law, but the law which at any moment is only an ideal, a law which is to be developed out of the present law:

> From this comes the defense and protection of your body and your life against neighbors, enemies, and murderers, and after that the protection and peace of your wife, daughters, son, house, estate, servants, money, property, land, and what you have: for all this is set down in the law, and walled and well fenced in. How great all this is, no one could ever describe in books. For who will express what an unspeakable asset blessed peace is? How much in one year alone does it give and spare?[85]

Human law has always two aspects:

1. Human law is the distribution of what is due to each person (*suum cuique,* "to each his own"). It is the determination of what I have the right to expect from others, and what others have a right to expect from me—of what I have a right to demand of others, and what they have a right to demand of me. *Aequitas* ("fairness," that which is "right and fair"), or reasonableness, is a decisive criterion for a law of which (as essential to law) it can be expected that it is not only externally observed by all the members of society but inwardly acknowledged. It must keep within the boundaries of the proportion that allows

the actions and the reactions to appear to some extent
equal. This gives assurance to everyone that nothing will
be demanded of him which goes beyond such acknowledged limits. Every transaction involving exchange (*Do
ut des,* "I give in order that you may give"), every
agreement on pay (equivalent for work done), has this
legal aspect, just as has every threat of punishment.

2. Every piece of legislation is at the same time a
permission—a guarantee of freedom. It defines a territory
within which I may move freely, it determines the
boundaries within which I have free disposal over my
property, within which I can move freely, express my
opinions freely, and freely join in organizing myself with
others. Under the security given by law I can move
freely, and that means, above everything else, without
fear. In the fifth Barmen thesis it is said of the state that it
has the task "in the as yet unredeemed world ... by
means of the threat and exercise of coercion ... to secure
law and peace." Both these concepts imply the concept
of freedom: Law is the granting of a sphere for free
individually responsible living. Where there was *only*
command and obedience, both freedom and law would
be absent; a slave has no law.

This second aspect of law has been less attended to in
the theological tradition than the securing of peace, that
is to say, of communal life, by law in the sense of the first
aspect. For this reason, and not only out of anxiety
concerning the political explosiveness of the concept,
the endeavor at the Barmen Synod of the Confessing
Church in May 1934 to mention the concept of freedom
along with the concepts of law and peace was not
successful. Within wide limits concerning what demands
could be made—limits mostly determined in the context
of natural law—it was considered the concern of the state
to determine what was each man's due. This view was
most consistently, and disastrously, held by the expo-

nents of legal positivism, which also denied the limits set by natural law. Fear of chaos led men to insist that unsatisfying or unreasonable decisions of the authorities must be accepted, and put up with, insofar as their change by the authorities could not be secured. But under no circumstances was illegal coercion to be opposed to legal coercion to achieve such changes.

Law as the protection of liberty is the fundamental axiom of all liberal tendencies in the field of law. "Better law" here means: more freedom, as much freedom of the individual as is possible without damage to the community and without injury to other lives. In any case, no one is to have less freedom than another; in a word, there is to be equality of rights. In our history, the liberal struggle for rights has found classical expression in the basic law of the Federal Republic of Germany.

If the theology of the great Christian confessions in our land so often acted as a brake, and only cooperated tardily and nervously, the chief reasons for this were twofold:

1. The pessimistic doctrine of man took more account of the deceptive power of sin and less account of the God-given powers of resistance against sin, and therefore less account of created reason and morality and the already effective power of the new life. Suspicion of man caused fear as to what he might do with his freedom, and made it seem advisable to grant him less rather than more freedom. In the defense of authoritarian structures there became evident at once the class-bound character of the pessimistic argument. Distrust was directed against the "rabble" (Luther), against the freedom of the masses, and ignored the fact that the ruling "rabble," the ruling class, share in an equal degree in sin and are in need of control just as much as the underdog.

2. The promise of liberation by the Holy Spirit for new life, as inner freedom which cannot be taken from us

even by chains and bondage, made men uninterested in efforts to obtain an external freedom. Freedom (singular) is decisive, but liberties are not! Further, this seemed to be legitimized by the New Testament's lack of interest in the liberation of slaves (I Cor. 7:20–24).

In the transformation of the apostle's pastoral advice to slaves into a general doctrine of the indifference of the gospel to outward freedom, admittedly class interests again became evident—with especially disastrous results in Luther's "Address to the Peasants." He did not see the close connection between outward and inner freedom; inner freedom can console us for the loss of outward freedom—the martyr in chains, the witness bravely facing death, is free in relation to the tyrant, his judges and executioners. This was the experience of primitive Christianity, and from it came the exhortation to the Christian slaves (especially fine is II Tim. 2:24ff.). No outward bondage can make us so captive that we do not have opportunities of service to others, even to those who oppress us, and consequently the responsibility of free men.

But inner freedom *longs* for outward freedom, for possibility of action, for external scope. And what a Christian longs for he must also grant to others and wish for them! This is the tendency toward *equality*, under the constraint of Christ's love: I cannot wish to have more than others, either of outward or inner possessions and possibilities.

And now if the principle *ora et labora* ("pray and work") holds good, I must also strive for what I wish as a Christian, and work for it, in political conflict for laws that give outward freedom. For laws can always give only outward, not inner freedom. The limit of outward freedom is the protection of togetherness; the freedom of my neighbor is the limit of my freedom; beyond this limit my freedom becomes coercion of others.

Political activity for the outward freedom as the freedom of all, not myself alone, is therefore a part of activity for better law. Therefore the removal of privilege which buttresses the inequality of bourgeois freedom is a goal of Christian participation in politics.

The two aspects of law—the *suum cuique* and the defense of liberty—belong inseparably together, and this knowledge led in modern times to the formulation of the ideals of *socialism*.

In the capitalist society both aspects are in appearance combined: the achievements of the bourgeois revolution are equality before the law and the individual rights of freedom, among them freedom of movement for those who were previously serfs, and freedom of work contract. Karl Marx exposed the specious character of this combination: The law gives to everyone the right to acquire the means of production and to produce with them—given that he has the necessary capital to do so. The law likewise gives everyone the right to sell his labor—given that this is his only capital. By so doing, it consolidates a fundamental inequality. With his labor power a man produces, but because he is not the owner of the means of production, he receives only so much of the product as he can extract from the owner, who, by reason of his ownership of the means of production, is the more powerful; and this transaction is dependent on the number of competitors who are selling their labor, and also upon the opposing power that can be developed by organizing the workers. But the pay which is thus secured by negotiation always remains far below the value of the goods produced. In addition, the seller of labor is excluded from something which cannot be estimated in terms of money, a privilege added to the ownership of the means of production, the freedom to decide about the conditions of work and the article which is produced. His *self*-determination is limited, by the lack of *co*determination, to what he can do with his pay. He produces collectively in the industry but is excluded from any say in the production, and thereby he is thrown back upon his isolated individual existence and so cannot find self-realization in a collective manner by active participation in a collective process of decision, as a true human being ought—according to a Christian understanding of life, which always regards life as an enterprise of fellowship.

No one in this system receives the *suum cuique,* neither the worker, who receives less than his due, and thus always an unjust payment, nor the owner of the means of production, who receives more than he ought, and thus always an unjust payment. And just as little does the whole of society receive the *suum cuique,* for society consists of more than those involved in production; it includes also the nonproducers, and these are not only those who by other types of service (ancillary services) contribute to keep production going, but also those who are weak in service, or incapable of it. If togetherness in equality of rights is the goal of Christian participation in the political conflict, then this goal as an ideal implies two things:

1. The whole system of production should serve the whole of society, in order to give equitably to all its members what they materially need for the maintenance of their lives. Here the weak are included, and also the coming generation, who are today in urgent need of guidance and care.

2. Within production the advantages of the owners of capital and the dependence of those who possess only their labor represent a situation of privilege which is reinforced by the coercive structure of society. Here the *suum cuique* is wanting, and consequently there is a failure to achieve justice, and also a failure to achieve freedom—just because of the lack of codetermination in the structuring of production. As long as the capitalist

system endures, the task for the political cooperation of Christians remains the replacement of the capitalistic life-style of society through legislation which removes these fundamental inequalities that hinder the social self-realization of all members of society. The result will not yet be the Kingdom of God, for it is still an order for sinners enforced by laws and by coercion. But it would be an order that realizes more togetherness and removes more privileges achieved by conflict than did the previous class society.

That is the perspective which irresistibly presents itself to me when I take the words "law and peace" in the Barmen Declaration and think them through consistently. In so doing, we have to defend the Fifth Thesis from the suggestion that it regards "the state," which has to care for law and order, as a hypostasis which hovers as an independent existence above human society. The tendency to such a viewpoint is present with us in undiminished force in a democratic guise, although it can no longer defend itself ideologically as the authorization "by God's grace" of persons in authority who represent this hypostatic state. We are the state. Although this fundamental proposition of the sovereignty of the people, the heart of democracy, has long been contested by theology (especially in Lutheranism and Catholicism), it is to be affirmed as Christian. For it gives the outward freedom for the realization of our responsibility in comprehensive codetermination and mutuality of control, which our universal sinfulness makes necessary. It hinders the hypostatization of the state, as if the latter were an entity that could be defined in itself in terms of some kind of metaphysical essence (a pretension which can always be unmasked as the expression of very concrete particular interests). The concrete state, however, is always defined by its laws, especially those laws which provide the fundamental limiting conditions for the individual laws, i.e., by its constitution. If the constitution secures the sovereignty of the people, and if this is so defined that it implies the free codetermination and cooperation of all in the processes of decision in society, then this constitution *is* the state, in which and through which we all provide for "law and peace."

This is easy to write. But in reality such a proposition covers a vast quantity of theoretical and historical problems. A constitution—whether written or not—is always the expression of a reality and an obligation. The reality of the constitution only corresponds to it in a limited degree. At least as important as its regulation of contemporary conditions is its character as a project directed to the future, as an "imperative" (as Gustav Heinemann used to say) of the fundamental law, as the setting forth of a task. The purpose of which I have spoken with reference to the cooperation of the Christian in society is to be recognized in the list of basic rights contained in the fundamental law. From this several things are apparent:

1. This fundamental law is made possible by modern humanism, which, as Paul Tillich has rightly said,[86] is a Christian humanism whether it knows it or not. It became possible against a cultural background in which Christian preaching was a decisive factor. Therefore the Christian purpose can be recognized in the modern humanistic purpose. Through the medium of humanism (and that of its most militant, aggressively advancing representative, Marxism) the purpose of the gospel for the earth and society is today making revolutionary advances over the whole terrestrial globe.

2. This Christian purpose is—thank God—not a special possession of Christians; it does not appeal only to Christians whose background is one of faith. Its plausibility extends far beyond the circle of the Christian community. Like good works (Matt. 5:16; I Peter 2:12, 15), the social purposes of the gospel have a prospect of

becoming universally acceptable, both as ideals and
utopias and also, when the time is ripe, as ideas for the
guidance of action and criteria for practice.

3. The sovereignty of the people, genuine democracy,
is not a present condition; it is not even distantly approached by a number of formal rules written into the
legal constitution, such as equality of suffrage and equality before the law. Such formal democracy is one step
toward the goal, but no more. It is possibly only a facade
behind which a quite different content may have free
scope to express itself. As yet there are no genuine
democracies in any country in our century. To compare
the reality behind the facade with the facade is the goal,
and at the same time it is a long process which demands
conflict, work, and time, great economic changes, profound changes in consciousness. The codetermination
and cooperation of all—that is an earthly utopia, a concrete, conceivable, and reachable goal, but one that will
take time to achieve, a goal that has received a first
incomplete anticipatory outline in the catalog of basic
rights contained in the fundamental law. No one knows
whether this goal will ever be more nearly approached
than in the highly contradictory phase of modern bourgeois democracy in which facade and actual facts,
"ought" and "is," are still so widely separated. No one
knows whether one day there will emerge from the
unhappy present state of development of the noncapital-
istic lands a greater approximation, a socialistic democracy, or whether shocking reverses will cause later genera-
tions to look on the contemporary approximation as a lost
dream. The progress of society toward the goal is by no
means certain, we cannot have faith in it, but we must
fight for it—especially as Christians, because what the
gospel says to us about the life of men together points us
in this "line and direction."[87]

The more our communal life in society approximates to

a real togetherness, and the more through solidarity—so far as laws can compel it and educate men toward it— they show *chesed,* solidarity, to each other, by that much more there comes into being an earthly horizon of grace for the earthly life of men, in a measure that is possible for them, and by that much more such a communal life will become a "parable" of the Kingdom of God, similar to it for all its dissimilarity. In that life men are exercised in an external behavior which corresponds to the togetherness of the new life: *magna similitudo in majore dissimilitudine* ("great similarity in greater dissimilarity"), according to the formula of the scholastic doctrine of analogy, which may be used in this context.

RECOMMENDED READING

Bahro, Rudolf. *Die Alternative. Zur Kritik des real existierenden Sozialismus.*

Heinemann, Gustav W. *Reden und Schriften.* Vol. 2: *Glaubensfreiheit—Bürgerfreiheit. Reden und Aufsätze zu Kirche—Staat—Gesellschaft 1945–1975.* 1976. Vol. 3: *Es gibt schwierige Vaterländer. Aufsätze und Reden 1949–1969.* 1977.

Mandel, Ernest. *Marxistische Wirtschaftstheorie.* 1970.

Sölle, Dorothee, and Schmidt, Klaus (eds.). *Christentum und Sozialismus. Vom Dialog zum Bündnis.* Urban-Taschenbücher, No. 609. 1974.

Sölle, Dorothee, and Schmidt, Klaus (eds.). *Christen für den Sozialismus. Analysen.* Urban-Taschenbücher, No. 613. 1975.

XII   Faith and Prayer

*Faith helps life, because it gives life an inexhaustible
meaning and makes it more difficult, because it is
mission and discipleship. The believer experiences certainty in a continually renewed search for the word of
Him who calls him. This search takes three forms:
prayer of petition, prayer of thanksgiving, and prayer of
adoration.*

Are things really easier for the believer? What things?
This life between birth and death, insecure, difficult,
anxious, endangered, aging, surrounded by death, mean-
ingless within horizons of decay. *Religion* appears as an
alleviation of life; it is recommended as such ("You'll
see, when things go hard with you, you will think
differently!"), and as such it is flayed by the criticism of
religion. All its positive aspects (the Father in heaven,
the love of God, redemption, resurrection, heaven) and
in addition the normative aspects (the commandments, a
final responsibility before God, judgment) show religion
and faith as a *help to life*. The question is only: *(a)*
whether it is a true help, and *(b)* whether it is really
helpful, or not rather a neurotic help to life and oneself
from which, for the sake of our healing, we must be free.
The two questions are *not* identical. Thus Nietzsche very
much questioned whether only the *truth* can make us
free (John 8:32—and many Freudians), or whether there
are not healthy, necessary lies about life, so that the task
of therapy is merely to replace the lies that make us ill
with healthy lies that will help us to cope with life. That
the *truth* is also *good* for us is a Christian proposition,
which depends on the presupposition that God is a life-
giving reality. The Enlightenment rejected the presup-

position about God but retained the proposition which it had inherited, taking it for granted as self-evident. But, as Nietzsche saw, this is by no means the case. It might well be that the truth is not tailored to suit us, nor we to suit it. It might well be that the truth is like Medusa's head, fatal to us (as Gottfried Benn often implies), so that we must conceal it from ourselves by the help of lies.

However that may be, these joyful utterances, which occur more frequently in the Christian faith than in other religions, cause faith to be regarded as a great alleviation of life, whether legitimate or illegitimate, and those who as atheists renounce the "consolation of religion" appear for that reason as heroes, of whom Christian apologetics is then accustomed to ask whether they are not taking too much upon themselves, because this demands superhuman powers, and whether they will not end in nihilism or despair—in which case religious people will then stand ready to catch them as they fall with the consolation of religion. This should not be treated ironically. But as a way of access to what faith and prayer in a biblical Christian context really mean, this common way of looking at things is too one-sided and anthropocentric, appealing too much to the mere needs of our weakness and destructive of our courage to face the truth, as Dietrich Bonhoeffer rightly saw.[88]

If we look at the Synoptic texts about discipleship and the autobiographical passages in Paul, things appear different. True, what surrounds Paul on the way to Damascus is light and not darkness, life-bestowing truth and not death, and his letters are pervaded with joy and gratitude for his becoming a participant in the new life. And in the Johannine letters it is the same. There is here no thought that these men should ever wish to renounce such "alleviation"—indeed, fulfillment of life. *But* there is here just as little illusion about the fact that discipleship and fellowship with Christ *make life difficult*. The

New Testament consistently gives as the reason for this the centrality of the *cross* of Jesus; the attack of the new life upon the old meets in us a resistance which brings to the new life deadly defeat. It has no prospect of meeting a joyful welcome and easily asserting itself, as might be conjectured from that first aspect (mankind in need of consolation, and rich consolation offered to it). No, on the contrary, the Savior is looked upon as an enemy and accordingly eliminated, and the attack is anything but a triumphal procession. The startling thing about John 1:11f. is that there are some who "received" him—but, according to the whole New Testament, not because in them the resistance of the old life was less, or because in them the good had not yet died, or because they had a better disposition for the new than many others, or because in contrast to the hardened sinners and atheists they were still accessible to a religious approach. No: they have received him because the new life—entirely through its own power—establishes itself in them, a fact by which they themselves are daily astonished. If that does not happen equally with all, it is "election," a special destiny, an advantage which then often enough— with appeals to obscure words of the Bible—has been thought of as a preferential selection for blessedness, according to which the *massa perditionis* ("the mass who are bound for perdition") go away empty and fall a prey to damnation. This is what makes the question of predestination so somber.

Here too Karl Barth's theology signifies a breakthrough from an old cul-de-sac: he understands election as a call to *mission*.[89] Contrary to a Christian egocentrism and egoistic views of salvation, election is to be understood as mission to others; it is for the sake of others that grace achieves its object with us. Here too the question "Why?" (i.e., "Why not with everyone uniformly?"), which must be postponed to the Last Day, and for which

we have *as yet no* answer, must be replaced by the
question "For what purpose?"—for which we certainly
must have an answer *today*. The answer of the New
Testament is: In order to propagate the new life in other
people and for other people.

But for this purpose and on this point the New Testament leaves us in no doubt: discipleship and fellowship
with Christ means nothing less than sharing in the way of
Jesus, and that is the way to the *cross* and through the
cross. Hence Paul's declaration in II Cor. 4:10 that he is
"always carrying in the body the death of Jesus." Hence
Paul's catalog of tribulations (Romans 8; I Corinthians 4;
II Corinthians 4; 6; 11; 12). The apostolic life is a life of
apostolic suffering. At this point a marginal note is
necessary. Neither does suffering as such receive a
positive accent, such as can be heard in some Christian
meditations on the Passion—either because of suffering
regarded as an end in itself or because of a religiously
disguised death instinct (Freud)—nor is the effort to
avoid or ward off suffering here repudiated. The motto of
the German Evangelical Kirchentag in Frankfurt am
Main in 1975, "As dying, and behold we live," is not
unobjectionable. It is taken from a Pauline catalog of
tribulations (II Cor. 6:4–9). Taken out of its context with
the apostolic sufferings there described, which can clearly be represented as a result of the apostolic service, such
a motto gives us the opportunity of speaking about all
sorts of anxieties of contemporary man, and of offering
the gospel as a help to peace of mind and an enhance-
ment of life; whereas it is necessary instead to ask for the
social causes of these anxieties which loom so large
today, and to inquire further about the possibilities of
removing these causes. It is precisely the man who under
the commandment of love takes part in the struggle
against these causes who is faced with such afflictions as
Paul here describes as the consequences, and it is then

for *this* situation that Jesus' promise holds good, "Lo, I have told you beforehand" (Matt. 24:25), which also must be related to the predictions of suffering contained in the words about discipleship (Mark 10:33f.; John 15:16–27).

Only here, in my opinion, do we grasp what the word *"faith"* really means—i.e., not primarily in the context of the *universal* situation of man, who longs for an alleviation of life, but in the context of the *special* situation of those particular men of whom, because of their special mission, a life of hardship is demanded. Thus we find the word "faith" in the Old Testament connected with the situation of Israel, and in the New Testament connected with the situation of the disciple and that of the church. Admittedly it is not limited to this, as is shown in the New Testament by figures like the centurion of Capernaum ("Not even in Israel have I found such faith," Matt. 8:10) and the Syrophoenician woman ("Great is your faith," Matt. 15:28). In their behavior the nature of faith becomes visible. But the reality that is faith is primarily necessary for the disciples, the chosen; without it they cannot move a step. To believe means—as precisely these two figures show—they put their trust in Jesus as in no other.

As soon as the word "faith" is mentioned we have continually to remind ourselves how very different its biblical meaning is from its general application in our everyday language. It does not mean a conjecture, something less certain than knowledge (Latin *putare:* "I believe that it will rain tomorrow"); nor does it mean the affirmation of ideas and assent to their truth, or assent to doctrinal systems and propositions ("I believe in progress in Marxism," etc.; "I believe that Jesus is God's Son"). The corresponding New Testament word *(pisteuein)* is only infrequently connected with a "that" clause (e.g., Heb. 11:3, 6); the corresponding Old Testament word cannot at all be so connected.[90] The Hebrew verbal root *emen* signifies "to be reliable, loyal" and (in a mood derived from it, Hiphil: *heemin*) "to support one-self upon, to rely upon." The substantives which derive from it *(emeth* and *emuna)* signify the solidarity of that on which one can rely, its loyalty and truth, or also, the firmness of reliance upon it, of trust. For this reason *fides* (Latin for "faith") in a biblical context must always be understood as *fiducia* ("trust").

On the other hand, in contrast with this, *pistis* in the New Testament includes both meanings of the Hebrew substantives, the (objective) reliability and loyalty of God, and the (subjective) reliance of the believer upon this loyalty. In his Short Exposition of the Confession of Faith of 1520,[91] in relation to the Latin word *credere,* Luther made a very beautiful distinction between the affirmation of existence *Credo Deum esse* ("I believe that God is"), and also the statement relating to God's utterances *Credo Deo* ("I believe him, God"), and the use of the word in the Apostles' Creed, *Credo in Deum* ("I believe in God"), which means, as he expounds it in his splendid paraphrase of the First Article of Faith (which cannot be too attentively studied): "I rely without conditions and limitations on him who has promised himself to me with all that he is, with all his divinity and power as Creator."

The additions to the word "God" in the First Article ("the almighty, creator of heaven and earth") do not give us doctrinal propositions which I need to affirm in an individual act of assent before I can rely on God, but they report how he who challenges me to unconditional trust describes himself in order that my trust should never come to an end.

Correspondingly, the words added to "Jesus Christ" in the Second Article are not individual Christological dogmas which demand to be affirmed in their own right, in order that faith may be complete. The truth is rather that they are used to describe and characterize the one in whose humanity the eternal God makes himself present to temporal, mortal, and guilty creatures, and gives himself for us; the additions describe the history in which that happened and the hope that it is meant to awaken in us. Of this Luther's exposition of the Second Article in his Small Catechism is a splendid paraphrase. It shows, moreover, that the selection of additions which the ancient church made in formulating the Apostles' Creed from the story of the Gospels is not necessarily obligatory for all time. It is thoroughly legitimate, and an act of Christian freedom, when contemporary formulations of the Christian faith, even for liturgical use, describe him whom Christians trust as their Lord with an emphasis laid upon other qualities ascribed to him by the New Testament.

Especially clear is the meaning of the additions in the Third Article. They give nothing but the works of the divine Spirit who is at the same time the Spirit of Jesus Christ, which we believe him to possess, and which we hope and ask to receive from him in whom we put our trust. For this reason it would be, for example, a mistake to repeat the word *in,* which stands next to *Spiritus Sanctus,* when speaking of the church, and to say *"Credo in ecclesiam"* (as has been proposed several times in modern Catholic ecclesiology); for we do not rely upon the church, but on the Holy Spirit, and have confidence in him that through him the Lord of the church will in all ages gather a church, maintain, unite, and renew it, and send it into the world.

In our everyday speech, "believe in" has also acquired the significance of a "that" proposition ("Do you believe in God?" = "Do you believe that it is true?"—or even merely: "Do you suppose that there is a God?"). Therefore this use of language must in every conversation about biblical and Christian matters be corrected by remembering that the *"Credo in . . ."* means: "I put in him and in his word my steadfast trust."

If I am to rely upon a person (not on a dumb thing like a bridge, or on a person as one would rely upon a thing), an action of personal approach to me must have preceded, a promise, a *word* in which this person commits himself to me. It is this *word* really on which my trust *relies* by directing itself to the person. If in this word we have at the same time to do with a task, a promise, *and* a command (gospel *and* law), then the promise answers for me those questions into which the mission leads me:

a. Does the matter have a good prospect of success? Are there chances of victory in spite of all defeats?

b. Am I to be left to my own devices? Have I got to make do with my own powers and means?

c. What will happen to me myself? Am I only a means to the end of the one who sends me? Am I to be expended on a wild-goose chase? Do I also arrive at the goal? Or is my part only to sacrifice myself in the good cause?

d. What will happen to me if, as is to be expected, I make mistakes, or even fail?

e. What will happen to me *and* the good cause, if it appears as if the one who has commissioned me withdraws himself, remains invisible, absent, and inactive?

These five questions describe the *temptation* of the disciple. They are already foreseen when the call is given, and because of them the task is from the beginning conjoined with the *promised answer* to each of the five questions. The author of the mission sends men commissioned into the conflict not unequipped with an answer to the questions which will come to them there, and his word that accompanies them reminds them continually not only of their task in the conflict but also of the promise, and challenges them to rely upon it, in order that they may fight against the questions of doubt that come to them; challenges them indeed to hold that this word is truer and more reliable than the evidence of their senses which call it into question. This accompanying promise is their most important weapon for the mission, and to lay hold of this weapon every day, that is *faith.*

We come to the following conclusions:

1. Faith is thus not a *condition* ("piety") but an act ever renewed; one does not have it, one does it, one lays hold of it again and again.

2. Faith is not a *world view* which one has acquired and defends against other ideologies. Ideologies can be useful as general orientations in the world. But faith does not make disclosures about the world; it is not conviction about the truth of a doctrinal system but trust in the one who has commissioned me, from person to person. All the Christian doctrines are, not assertions to be regarded as true in themselves, but only descriptions of the one who has commissioned us, and of his actions, in order to justify and underline our trust in him.

3. Faith cannot be established as present in me by introspection. It is precisely a looking away from myself to the other, whom I urgently need if I am not to fail in the mission. It is the contrary of a gaze directed inward upon myself. So Paul Althaus is right when he says, "I do not know if I believe, but I do know in whom I believe."[92] And Karl Barth is right also when he says: "We cannot believe in our *faith*. And we can also only *believe* in our faith."[93]

4. Faith, as we have shown, is itself action, a grasping, the one good work in which all other good works are based (Luther). For how could the sender be pleased with an accomplishment of his mission in which the one sent emancipates himself from the sender, and in self-willed and Promethean confidence takes the matter into his own hands? If he thinks that he does not need the

help of the sender, then he will soon go on to believe that he understands the *commission* better than the sender; his self-confidence will relate also to the interpretation of the commission, and he will change it to suit his own pleasure. Of this kind of thing church history gives plenty of evidence.

5. Faith is not only itself an action, but it is always bound up with the rest of our action and behavior. We do not first perform a special action, called faith, in our inwardness, and then set about an external action, the fulfillment of the commission. When Luther says that faith is the first work,[94] he does not mean that chronologically it precedes other action. He means, rather, that it accomplishes itself in, with, and under our external action, our activity in obeying the commission. *The very fact* that Peter, in obedience to Jesus' word, at the wrong time sails out into the deep water of the lake, an unlikely place for a catch of fish, is an act of faith (Luke 5:1–11). *The very fact* that the sick man at the pool of Bethesda does not wait until he feels a stream of power flowing through his limbs, but, without the experience of his senses, gets up in obedience to Jesus' word, thus doing what he cannot do, is an act of faith (John 5:1–9). It is not before, but in the very act of continually laying hold of Jesus' commission, that we continually lay hold of Jesus' promise. This is expressed in Luther's distinctions, which belong together: *Fides sola justificat, sed numquam est sola* ("Faith alone justifies, but it is never alone"). Faith is the agent, love is the action.

6. Promises always belong to the *future*. This was Israel's interpretation of the name of God, the tetragram YHWH. "He who said 'I will be with you' has sent me to you" (Ex. 3:14). This trust is *hope*, hope for the hopeless sheep among the wolves.[95]

This brings us to the identity of *faith* and *prayer*. If faith is an action, namely the reaching out of the one who has been sent, to the promise of the sender, then this is nothing other than *prayer*. For it is an answering with words—either merely silent or spoken out loud: "I hear that. I will rely on it. I will continue to build on your word, and do what you say."

And so these five questions we have mentioned are *questions of faith*. When I address them to the sender, and allow myself to be answered by hearing and grasping his promises, I continue to act on the basis of faith. If I address them to others, in order to learn from others if the prospects are favorable, if my abilities and powers will be adequate, or if I myself will come to grief in the project—then my questions are not questions of faith, but of pure doubt, in which I allow myself to be encouraged or depressed by others, and in which at best I put my trust in other people and other circumstances. This will certainly not make me more efficient for the mission, but less efficient. So even Job's questions are questions of faith; for he directs them with all the violence of his complaint to no other person than God, his God, and will have no one answer them but this God of his. The same is true of Jesus' question in Gethsemane, and of his cry of dereliction on the cross. It is not asking questions of God and disputing with God that is faithless; trust can take even this shape, so long as in questioning and disputing it appeals to the promise and asks for its fulfillment, as often happens in The Psalms.

And this gives an answer to the doubts cast on the question about the legitimacy of petitionary prayer, a theme dealt with in modern times in theology. In the face of modern knowledge about the rule of law in the events of nature, and also the incredibility of the traditional unbiblical conception of *miracle* (miracle as an infringement of natural laws), petitionary prayer became a problem, because it seemed to require just such an infringement. For an *intervention* by God of this kind the natural system allows no gaps, according to the modern conception of natural law, and the modern methods of controlling nature seem to us to replace what petitionary prayer expects of God. Even the farmer who prays for a blessing on the crop does not renounce the use of artificial fertilizers and modern scientific methods of farming, and thus he apparently refutes his prayer as a superfluous ritual carried over from the past.

If in spite of this there was a wish to retain prayer, then it was frequently reduced to worship—the pure praise of God, which asks nothing of him but merely honors him—and, if need be, to a prayer of *thanksgiving* which is grateful for God's gifts and love. But these were an inconsistency, for one who only rules from his throne above us, and does not care about us, would be indifferent both to our prayers and to our worship, and therefore not worthy of our worship. The Creator whom we thank is not worthy of our thanks, if in our need he leaves us in the lurch, and if he does not hear our prayers. Worship, prayers of thanksgiving, and prayers of petition belong inseparably together and only have meaning when taken together.

So faith and prayer only have meaning if they rely upon the promise of God who intervenes and can intervene. The intervention of God only became a problem because it was too closely connected with the thought of gaps and interruptions—in the way that we, for example, in order to parry a saber thrust, interrupt one causal chain by means of another causal chain that we initiate. But here we must take note that even in this case of a human intervention, a gap in natural events is not taken advantage of, nor is the causal connection interrupted. What we do is, rather, to use it, and the causal connection is of service to our intervening will. So, concerning God's intervention, the question is not where and how we can conceive of it (every conception of the manner of it must be avoided), but whether we believe that God has a will, or whether it seems too anthropomorphic to think of God as will. And here we have returned again to the question that arose earlier. If we inquire about God in a metaphysical manner, i.e., from finitude seeking the infinite, from the conditioned seeking the unconditioned, then all affirmative statements appear too anthropomorphic, and we never get beyond limiting concepts. But if we inquire about God on the basis of definite experiences—and in our case, on the basis of the experiences of Israel and the disciples—then our inquiry will be directed toward him whose urgent reality is here experienced as one that challenges those on whom it presses, and whom it "chooses," setting them in movement, changing them, and sending them. If we speak of God's reality, as we ought and may, in human language, then the word *"will"* becomes inevitable and essential to describe this reality. It is not a mere idea, a vision, a utopia, that takes possession of us and draws us into the dangerous adventure of attacking present conditions in their inhumanity, the old for the sake of the new, but a will greater than ours that draws us into its enterprise, brings us to desert from the force of those who "did not receive him" (John 1:11) and to enter into the band of those who do receive him. We *thank* this will for our being given a share in the conflict of the new, true, good life, against the life of death (an intentionally paradoxical word describing the life that is in love with death and killing); to him we pray, to him we sing hymns of adoration, as the light that encircles us, glad that through his word the things that cannot be taken for granted are made secure and certain. The final truth is not death, but life and light for us. We trust that this will desires to intervene, and that it can intervene, and as those under commission we *pray* for this, because without it, and left to our own resources, we cannot for a moment keep ourselves on the side of the new life and be useful for it. "Without me you can do nothing" (John 15:5). So the *prayer of petition*—beginning from the central *"Veni, creator spiritus!"* down to the smallest, even the most external problem of the day— is a natural mode of the life of disciples, an appropriate form of their life in unbroken conversation with him who sends them, their *oratio continua* (I Thess. 5:17), their "prayer without ceasing."

The communication between God and man is *human*, i.e., expressed in language, not in the tongues of angels, taking place in a superhuman sphere, and not only in powerful influences, feelings, psychical thrills, something less than human. The two partners in this *conversation* are capable of communication, thanks to the promise which comes through human messengers in human words. The whole of mankind has hoped for this, for it has always prayed, movingly, even in words that can be adopted by disciples. That is not, as has been objected in the past, an argument that prayer, because not specifically Christian, might be superfluous for Christians, nor is it an argument for prayer being merely the mythological form of *meditation*, regarded as the true unmythological essence of prayer, i.e., self-reflection and absorption in the depths of the self and the universe.[96] These are all attempts to save something of prayer without the *confrontation* in which it takes place, because—it is argued in terms of the metaphysical inquiry about God—in such confrontation no person who could be addressed becomes either visible or audible.

This is what makes prayer today so hard to accept, and for many almost impossible to engage in, surrounded as it is by countless questions. Who is being spoken to when someone speaks with God? Into what darkness is one's voice dissipated? Where is there any prospect, any proof of its being heard and received? Roger Garaudy said to me in a discussion in 1971, "We atheists have been given no assurance, no promise, no covenant . . . , and no one expects us."[97] We live in brotherhood with such atheists, working together with them, where we and they—from whatever cause—see steps being taken in the direction of a new togetherness in life instead of the old deathly life of conflict; but we are invited and empowered, by the word that daily reaches us and challenges us, to say for ourselves and for them: A new life is assured to us, we have great promises, we are in a covenant that presses forward urgently, and we are expected.

RECOMMENDED READING

Cardenal, Ernesto. *Zerschneide den Stacheldraht! Südamerikanische Psalmen.* 3d ed. 1968.
Ebeling, Gerhard. *Vom Gebet. Predigten über das Vaterunser.* 1963.
Guardini, Romano. *Vorschule des Betens.* 1948.
Miskotte, Kornelis Heiko. *Der Weg des Gebets.* 1964.
Sölle, Dorothee. *Sympathie. Theologische-politische Traktate.* 1978.

Epilogue

Who expects us, and what awaits us? What awaits us is today written in letters of flame on the horizon of this epoch by its prophets of apocalypse, Gordon R. Taylor and Günter Anders, Robert Jungk and Wolfgang Harich and all the rest. Whether the end or a turning point is before us[98] no one can as yet know, and the end seems more probable when we consider the inconceivable blindness with which the people in power in state, society, and industry turn a deaf ear to all warnings, and, confronted by a unique threat posed to the existence of mankind and its basis in nature by us men, continue to pursue the struggle for their particular interests, their imperialisms, and the mad armaments race, as they have done in the past, driving us every day nearer to destruction.

We are all caught in this trap, as nations and as individuals. The citizen of the United States of America, so far as he does not belong to the millions that live under the minimum subsistence level, affirms in practice the hunger and undernourishment of millions of children in Latin America, since his prosperity is made possible by the iron fetters in which the United States holds this unhappy continent captive. We Germans are just as much implicated by our business concerns and our politics in the exploitation and pollution of the other continents, and each of us in practice affirms this situation by the daily enjoyment of his privileges at the expense of those who are going hungry through our fault. In practice, by our need for security, by our electoral votes for our parties that support armament, we are all affirming the creation, stockpiling, further development, and threat of mass weapons of human destruction such as the world has never yet seen. While the attention of our

221

population is distracted by acts of terror committed by misguided groups, there hangs over us the Damoclean sword of a terroristic potential of annihilation for which no divine law, and therefore no earthly law, has given permission or mandate. Protesting against totalitarianism in other parts of the world, we are living today under the totalitarian compulsion of deadly armaments. We affirm in practice the godless production of the poison plutonium, which has been invented by us, and is not to be found in nature—over 40,000 kilograms every year—which we have now incorporated into world history for hundreds of thousands of years to come. We agree to this production of plutonium because of our expenditure of energy, which justifies it, according to the claims of the powers that be.

We are so entangled in our complicity, and so ineffectual in our resistance, that even those who see clearly are only able to go on living by frequently shutting their eyes to what they see. In our daily cares, joys, and occupations we accept the world as if it were still the same as it has always been, and yet the world is right on the edge of the abyss. We are all like the Pompeian housewife, in a drawing of the Italian caricaturist G. Novello, who on the morning before the eruption of Vesuvius insists that her maids should thoroughly dust her ornaments. Even the churches, which possess in their Bible the Apocalypse of John, and which in the face of this keep silent or else find only tired noncommittal words for it, are like this housewife in their daily church activities, as are the professional but naive theologians. All this is happening at a level far below what the hour demands, and bears no relation to what the apocalyptic prospect of the destruction of mankind requires of us.

Even in this book it is hardly noticeable how much the situation was in my mind when, for example, I was dealing with the "life of death" or the self-destruction of sin, which the divine project of salvation opposes. Now, at the last moment, it must be clearly stated that every-thing that has been said about the gospel is profoundly called into question by the situation of mankind today, and that it is precisely under this challenge that the promise of the gospel makes itself heard, and proposes to set us on our feet again and to make us work for a mankind that threatens to commit suicide. The dispro-portion between the apparent weakness of this promise and the gigantic might of the powers of annihilation is the same disproportion that exists between the Crucified One and the might of those for whose political game he is only an insignificant pawn. It is the same disproportion too as that in which the hearers of the gospel constantly found themselves when confronted by the murder and violence around them which they could not prevent. If, at the end of Chapter IV, the message of the resurrection was contrasted with the "pessimism of destruction" which world conditions today so strongly suggest, the intention was not in the least to make light of this pessimism of destruction, or to deny that it was right and reasonable. It is a realistic view of the matter. But just for that reason it is impossible any longer to prevail against the hopelessness resulting from all realistic analyses of the world situation today, and the paralysis which results from it, with anything less than the message of the resurrection. Not that we are to console ourselves for the threatening destruction with the inalienable prospect of eternal life that is ours beyond the grave, and to leave this world to its fate. That would be an egoistic consola-tion, which in addition overlooked the fact that every one of us has a share in the responsibility for this fate. It is a legitimate consolation only when it helps us to overcome that paralysis and to take up anew the struggle for the salvation, in history, of this world, which is God's be-loved creation. It is a legitimate consolation when pity for those who are daily sacrificed to the powers of destruction drives us to place ourselves by the side of the victims, and to repudiate our complicity with the powers of destruction.

How each of us *in* the entanglement can bestir himself and work actively *against* the entanglement, and replace previous solidarity with the agents of destruction by solidarity with the victims, and thus also with the overall victim, with mother earth, from whom we draw our life— for this no general prescriptions can be given. In daily practice, in conversation between the disciples of Jesus and their clear-sighted contemporaries, the ways for this must be sought, and every moment of time that is still left us is a respite of grace, of which we must take advantage with all our powers. What I have set forth is an attempt to describe the equipment which the gospel gives us for our practical life in this respite of grace: motive, criteria, fellowship in the divine covenant, power of endurance, line and direction—and hope, where there seems nothing more to hope for.

Therefore the question of what awaits us is enclosed in the question, Who awaits us? It is the God of the resurrection, who brings life to us in our suicidal madness, and who asks us again and again, "Why will you die?" (Ezek. 18:31; 33:11; Jer. 27:13). He, for whom we wait when our time here is at an end, waits for us here right to the last moment. So I close with the significant story which Gustav Heinemann told when he concluded his term of office:

In the middle of the last century in the North American Middle West a state legislature was in session. A terrible storm, as happens in that district, gathered, and darkened the heavens. It grew as black as night, and the end of the world seemed at hand. The members were filled with terror and wanted to break off the session and rush out of the council chamber. The speaker of the legislature

called to them: "Gentlemen: either the end of the world
has not yet come, and our Lord is not yet coming—in that
case there is no reason for breaking off the session. Or our
Lord is coming now—then let him find us at work. The
session will continue."[99]

Notes

1. Johann Gottlieb Fichte, *Erste Einleitung in die Wissenschaftslehre* (1797), *Sämtliche Werke* (1845), Vol. 1, p. 434.

2. Instructive on this point is Paul Feyerabend, *Wider den Methodenzwang—Entwurf einer anarchistischen Erkenntnistheorie* (Frankfurt, 1976).

3. Cf. the discussion and debate between Wilhelm Weischedel and myself in *Denken und Glauben* (Stuttgart, 1964), and my reaction to Weischedel's work *Der Gott der Philosophen. Grundlegung einer philosophischen Theologie im Zeitalter des Nihilismus*, 2 vols. (Darmstadt, 1971; Munich, 1972²), under the title " 'Der Gott der Philosophen' und die Theologie," in *Denken im Schatten des Nihilismus. Festschrift für W. Weischedel zum 70. Geburtstag*, ed. by A. Schwan (Berlin, 1975), pp. 375–401. Karl Barth himself was not satisfied with his attempt to define the boundaries in his essay "Philosophie und Theologie," in *Philosophie und christliche Existenz. Festschrift für Heinrich Barth zum 70. Geburtstag am 3.2.1960* (Basel/Stuttgart, 1960), pp. 93–106.

4. For the distinction between these two forms of atheism, see my Berlin Introductory Lecture, "Die Theologie im Hause der Wissenschaften," *Evangelische Theologie*, Vol. 18 (1958), pp. 14–37.

5. Werner Jaeger, *Die Theologie der frühen griechischen Denker* (1953), pp. 12ff. Cf. also Karl Kerényi in *Kerygma und Mythos*, VI/1 (Hamburg, 1963), pp. 29f., and Ferdinand Kattenbusch, "Die Entstehung einer christlichen Theologie," in *Zeitschrift für Theologie und Kirche*, 1930, pp. 161–205 (reprint, *Wissenschaftliche Buchgesellschaft*, Darmstadt, 1962).

6. Jaeger, *Die Theologie der frühen griechischen Denker*, p. 13.

7. Wolfhart Pannenberg, *Wissenschaftstheorie und*

Theologie (Frankfurt, 1973). E.T. *Theology and the Philosophy of Science* (Philadelphia, 1976).

8. Adolf von Harnack, *Das Wesen des Christentums* (1900). E.T. *What Is Christianity?* (1901).

9. It is well known that Dietrich Bonhoeffer in his *Widerstand und Ergebung* (E.T. *Letters and Papers from Prison*, p. 148; London, 1953) described Karl Barth's theology of revelation as "positivism of revelation." This was certainly a mistake. The misunderstanding is, however, as natural as it is momentous—and this is important if one is to read Barth's writings with understanding, since only by avoiding it will one achieve a true understanding of Barth. That Bonhoeffer at that time could so misunderstand him is, in my opinion, due to the fact that in this criticism of Barth he was critically breaking free from his own earlier period and his own earlier interpretation of Barth. Cf. my contribution to *Begegnungen mit Dietrich Bonhoeffer*, ed. by Wolf-Dieter Zimmermann, 4th enlarged ed. (Munich, 1969), pp. 109–116.

10. Ludwig Feuerbach, *Pierre Bayle. Ein Beitrag zur Geschichte der Philosophie und Menschheit* (Kröner-Ausgabe), pp. 19f.

11. Weischedel, *Der Gott der Philosophen*, Vol. 1, p. 1.

12. Cf. Walter Dirks, *Alte Wörter. Vier Kapitel zur Sprache der Frömmigkeit* (Munich, 1976).

13. Cf. Martin Kähler, *Die Wissenschaft der christlichen Lehre* (1883; new ed. 1966, p. 33): "The revelation of God aims not at an act of knowledge, but a living fellowship with God; therefore it is really understood only when it is apprehended as presently operative." Karl Barth, "Offenbarung, Kirche, Theologie," *Theologische Existenz heute*, No. 9 (1934): "Knowledge of revelation does not mean knowledge of an abstract God in confrontation with an abstract man, but knowledge of the concrete God, who has sought out man, in confrontation with the concrete man who is found by God. It is knowledge of God and of men made concrete in the event of God's initiative from above" (p. 19). "Revelation

means: God himself is here, where we are, with us in the same way that we are; nay, he is what we are" (p. 22).

14. Cf. Karl Barth, "Der Christ als Zeuge," *Theologische Existenz heute*, No. 12 (1934), and "Die Grundformen des theologischen Denkens," *Evangelische Theologie*, Vol. 3 (1936), pp. 462ff., reprinted in *Theologische Fragen und Antworten. Gesammelte Vorträge*, Vol. 3 (1957), pp. 282–290.

15. Pannenberg, *Wissenschaftstheorie und Theologie*, p. 336. Pannenberg indeed sees himself as in opposition to Barth. His polemic against Barth is concentrated on Barth's sharp rejection of Heinrich Scholz's postulate for a theology which claims scientific character: "Wie ist evangelische Theologie als Wissenschaft möglich?" *Zwischen den Zeiten*, 1931, pp. 8–53, reprinted in *Theologie als Wissenschaft*, ed. by Gerhard Sauter, pp. 221–264, Theologische Bücherei, No. 43 (Munich, 1970); cf. Barth's *Kirchliche Dogmatik*, I/1, p. 7. E.T. *Church Dogmatics*, I/1 (Edinburgh, 1936), pp. 7–8.

Pannenberg hears only Barth's "No!" and consequently reads Barth's propositions as if they were proclaiming a type of thought that takes heed of no rules of logic, intelligibility, and demonstration, and insists—as if this were necessary in confronting Barth—that even a theological book must be reasonable and intelligible (Pannenberg, *Wissenschaftstheorie und Theologie*, p. 277). Haunted by this one page at the beginning of the *Kirchliche Dogmatik*, Pannenberg has not seen that in the volumes of this great work—as in my opinion can be demonstrated—Barth in general completely satisfies Scholz's postulates, and, where this is not the case, gives a reason for not doing so. He has not repudiated their relevance for orderly thought, but only as *a priori* conditions which do not leave theology the freedom, in terms of the superior postulate of practical relevance (which Barth proclaims as the only binding postulate), to satisfy these other postulates, or sometimes not, in each case knowing and giving reasons for what it does.

16. John Calvin, *Institutio Religionis Christianae*, I.

vi. 2: Omnis recta cognitio Dei ab obedientia nascitur.

17. Adolf Schlatter, *Der Dienst des Christen in der älteren Dogmatik* (1897), pp. 18–22, chapter: "Die passive Gemeinde."

18. André Gorz, *Ökologie und Politik* (Reinbek, 1977), No. 4120, pp. 125f.

19. K. Marti, "Entfremdung und Erfahrung in Theologie und Literatur," in *Grenzverkehr* (Neukirchen, 1976), p. 95.

20. Paulo Freire, in *Brüderlichkeit—die vergessene Parole*, ed. by H. J. Schulz (Stuttgart, 1976), p. 105.

21. Ernesto Cardenal, *Das Evangelium der Bauern von Solentiname*, Vol. 1 (Wuppertal, 1976).

22. On this point, see Karl Barth, *Die protestantische Theologie im 19. Jahrhundert* (Munich, 1947), p. 277. E.T. *Protestant Theology in the Nineteenth Century* (London, 1972), pp. 310–311.

23. Weischedel, *Der Gott der Philosophen*, Vol. 2 (Munich, 1972²), p. 58.

24. Formula of Concord (1579), in Philip Schaff, *The Creeds of Christendom*, Vol. 2, pp. 93–94.

25. Karl Marx, *Zur Kritik der Hegelschen Rechtsphilosophie*, in *Frühschriften*, ed. by S. Landshut (Stuttgart, 1958), p. 217.

26. Karl Barth, *Einführung in die evangelische Theologie* (Zurich, 1962), p. 40.

27. Ibid.

28. This is the program suggested for it by Ernst Bloch in *Atheismus im Christentum. Zur Religion des Exodus und des Reichs* (Frankfurt, 1973).

29. Quoted, with other subjects, in G. Heidtmann, ed., *Glaube im Ansturm der Zeit. Zeugnisse und Manifeste der evangelischen Kirche aus den Jahren 1933–1967*, Stundenbücher, No. 78 (Hamburg, 1968), pp. 31ff.

30. *D. Martin Luthers Werke. Kritische Gesamtausgabe* (Weimar, 1883ff.), WA, 16, 111, 7. Hereafter cited as WA.

31. Karl Barth, *Dogmatik im Grundriss* (Stuttgart, 1947), pp. 93–94. E.T. *Dogmatics in Outline* (1949).

32. Luther, WA, Letters 2, 397 (Letter of 1.11.1521): *Germanis meis natus sum, quibus et serviam.*

33. Rudolf Bultmann, *Das Verhältnis der urchristlichen Christusbotschaft zum historischen Jesus* (Reports of the Sessions of the Heidelberg Academy of Sciences, 1960), p. 9.

34. Martin Buber, *Ich und Du* (Heidelberg, 1974[8]), p. 132. E.T. *I and Thou* (1937).

35. Luther in the exposition of the First Commandment in his Large Catechism.

36. Xenophanes of Colophon (ca. 570–475 B.C.) lived an unsettled, wandering life as singer and poet, especially in Sicily. Some of his themes were important, new, and influential in later times, especially his criticism of the mythology in Homer and Hesiod.

37. Weischedel, *Der Gott der Philosophen*, Vol. 2.

38. This is the definition of God in the so-called ontological proof of the existence of God, in the *Proslogion* of Anselm of Canterbury (1033–1109).

39. Cf. Kornelis Heiko Miskotte, *Wenn die Götter schweigen. Vom Sinn des alten Testaments* (Munich, 1963).

40. Democritus, Greek philosopher, ca. 460–360 B.C.

41. Martin Buber, *Die Chassidischen Bücher* (1928), pp. XIf.

42. "To all" was the address inscribed on the telegram of the October Revolution of 1917; it was intended for the whole human race.

43. Rudolf Otto, theologian and historian of religions (1869–1937), in his book *Das Heilige* (1917). E.T. *The Idea of the Holy*.

44. Paul Tillich, *Systematische Theologie*, Vol. 1 (Stuttgart, 1955). E.T. *Systematic Theology*, Vol. 1 (London: Nisbet, 1953), Part II, II B.

45. F. Wedekind, "Aufschrei," in *Die vier Jahreszeiten, Winter, Gesammelte Werke*, Vol. 1 (1920), p. 117.

46. Barth, *KD*, I/1, p. 404. E.T. I/1, p. 441.

47. Barth, *KD*, I/2, pp. 348ff. E.T. I/2, pp. 318–319.

48. Ernst Bloch, *Atheismus im Christentum.*

49. Barth, *KD*, III/3, p. 193. E.T. III/3, p. 171.

50. So E. Wolff, "Häresie," RGG[3], Vol. 3, III, Sp. 14.

51. Hans Ehrenberg, a German, Jewish-Christian theologian (1883–1958), in his pamphlet *Die Sünde im öffentlichen Leben. Ein Wort von der sozialen Bekehrung.* Also *Der Heilsweg im öffentlichen Leben. Ein Wort der Vorbereitung auf die Bekehrung der Kirche.* Der Kampf-Bund, Vols. 6 and 7 (1927, 1928).

52. Marcion, an early Christian Gnostic, repudiated by the church (ca. A.D. 150). See also Chapter V.

53. Into this prayer, the Shemoneh Esreh, which the pious Jew was supposed to pray three times a day, there was inserted about the end of the first century A.D. the so-called Birkath ha-minim: "May the Nosrim (Nazarenes = Jewish Christians) and Minim (heretics, backsliders) come quickly to ruin." Cf. Jakob Jodz, *The Jewish People and Jesus Christ: A Study in the Controversy Between Church and Synagogue* (London, 1954), pp. 51–57.

54. Friedrich Nietzsche, *Werke* (Edition Schlechta, Munich, 1965), Vol. 1, p. 1068.

55. Adolf von Harnack, *Marcion. Das Evangelium vom fremden Gott* (Leipzig, 1920), p. 217.

56. Arthur Koestler, *Der dreizehnte Stamm. Das Reich der Khasaren und sein Erbe* (Munich, 1977).

57. Cf. Hendrik Berkhof, *Kirche und Kaiser* (1947).

58. Cf. Karl Thieme, "Augustinus und der ältere Bruder. Zur patristischen Auslegung von Luk 15.25–32," in *Universitas. Festschrift für Bischof A. Stöhr* (1960), Vol. 1, pp. 79–85.

59. Cf. Karl Barth, *Humanismus,* Theologische Studien, No. 28 (1950). Also *Die Menschlichkeit Gottes,* Theologische Studien, No. 48 (1956).

60. Karl Barth, "Gottes Wille und unsere Wünsche," in *Theologische Existenz heute,* No. 7 (1934), pp. 16–30.

61. Hans-Joachim Kraus, *Reich Gottes—Reich der Freiheit. Grundriss systematischer Theologie* (Neukirchen, 1975), p. 124.

62. Martin Buber, "Der heilige Weg" (1919), in *Reden über das Judentum* (Berlin, 1932[2]), p. 164.

63. Karl Barth, "Christengemeinde und Bürgergemeinde" (1946), last printed in Theologische Studien, No. 104 (1970).

64. Kraus, *Reich Gottes—Reich der Freiheit*, p. 409.

65. Leonhard Ragaz would "have preferred to give the title 'The World Revolution' " to his book *Die Botschaft vom Reiche Gottes* (Bern, 1942). Cf. his letter to Martin Buber of 1.28.1942, in Buber, *Correspondence*, Vol. 3, p. 57.

66. Compare on this point A. von Harnack's thesis on the Hellenization of Christianity.

67. Karl Marx, *Die Frühschriften*, ed. by S. Landshut (Stuttgart, 1971[6]), p. 246.

68. Erasmus of Rotterdam, *Diatribe de libero arbitrio* (1524).

69. Martin Luther, *De servo arbitrio* (1525).

70. Johann Wolfgang von Goethe, *Torquato Tasso* I, 1, V. 106.

71. "O day of wrath, that dreadful day," the beginning of the sequence in the Mass on All Souls' Day.

72. Cf. J. H. Pestalozzi, "They drown righteousness in the cesspool of grace." Quoted from *Sämtliche Werke* (Berlin, 1938), Vol. 12, p. 56.

73. Karl Marx, *Frühe Schriften*, ed. by H.-J. Lieber and P. Furth (1962), Vol. 1, pp. 21f. Cf. on this point J. M. Lochman, *Christus oder Prometheus? Die Kernfrage des christlich-marxistischen Dialogs und die Christologie*, Furche-Stundenbücher (1972), p. 106.

74. Barth, *KD*, II/2, p. 776. E.T. II/2, p. 695.

75. Cf. Walter Kreck, *Grundfragen der Dogmatik*, 2d enlarged ed. (Munich, 1977), esp. pp. 89, 151ff.

76. Article on the Communion from Luther's Small Catechism. In the Latin version (*Die Bekenntnisschriften der Evangelisch-Lutherischen Kirche*, p. 520; 1930, 1956[3]): *Ubi enim remissio peccatorum est, ibi est et vita et justitia.*

77. Hans Küng, *Rechtfertigung* (Einsiedeln, 1957), p. 257. E.T. *Justification* (London and Philadelphia, 1964, 1981).

234   Notes

78. Augustine, *De doctrina Christiana* I.1.1, in *Corpus Christianorum, Series Latina XXXII*, 6: *Omnis enim res, quae dando non deficit, dum habetur et non datur, nondum habetur, quomodo habenda est.*

79. Hermann Cohen, *Der Begriff der Religion im System der Philosophie* (1915), quoted by Martin Buber, *Gottesfinsternis* (Heidelberg, 1953), p. 67. E.T. *Eclipse of God* (London, 1953), p. 77.

80. Karl Barth, *Christliche Ethik* (Munich, 1946), pp. 10f.

81. Bertolt Brecht, *Dreigroschenoper,* in *Werkausgabe* Edition Suhrkamp (Frankfurt am Main), Vol. 2, p. 458.

82. *The Communist Manifesto,* in Marx-Engels, *Ausgewählte Schriften* (Berlin, 1968), Vol. 1, p. 26.

83. As an example I mention Walter Künneth's political ethic, *Politik zwischen Gott und Dämon* (Hamburg, 1952), and the discussion started by the Catholic bishops since their opposition to a new regulation of paragraph 218, dealing with "Fundamental Value." This is set forth, instead of the admittedly very necessary discussion about the fundamental rights of citizens and their preservation and further development, with the purpose of binding the state to fundamental ordinances defined by the church.

84. Karl Barth, *Christengemeinde und Bürgergemeinde* (Munich, 1946), reprinted in Theologische Studien, No. 104 (1970), pp. 65f.

85. Martin Luther, *Sämtliche Werke* (Erlangen, 1829), pp. 20, 28.

86. Paul Tillich, *Kirche und humanistische Gesellschaft* (1931), reprinted in *Gesammelte Werke*, Vol. 9 (Stuttgart, 1975), pp. 47–81.

87. Barth, *Christengemeinde und Bürgergemeinde*, p. 60.

88. Bonhoeffer, *Widerstand und Ergebung,* new ed. (Munich, 1970), pp. 356ff. E.T. *Letters and Papers from Prison* (London, 1953), pp. 158–159.

89. Barth, *KD,* IV/3, pp. 650ff. E.T. IV/3, pp. 566ff.

90. This difference has misled Martin Buber, in *Zwei*

Glaubensweisen (1953), into the construction of an essential difference between faith in the Old Testament and in Paul—a certainly untenable thesis.

91. Martin Luther, *Eine kurze Form der Zehn Gebote, des Glaubens und des Vaterunsers*, WA 7, pp. 215f.

92. This good sentence I remember hearing from Paul Althaus (1930), but cannot at the moment give a reference in his writings. Cf. on this point Paul Althaus, *Theologische Aufsätze* (1929), Vol. 1, pp. 95f.: "Faith is movement *in itself*. One believes by repeatedly laying hold of faith. One holds God's hand by continually laying hold of it. One lives in God only by continually fleeing to him."

93. Karl Barth, *Ethik II* (1928/29), ed. D. Braun (Zurich, 1978), p. 29.

94. Martin Luther, *Sermon von den guten Werken* (1520), WA 6, p. 204: "The first and highest, noblest good work of all is faith in Christ. . . . For all works must go into this work and receive the influence of their goodness, as it were a loan from it."

95. Chr. Gestrich, *Homo peccator und homo patiens*, *Zeitschrift für Theologie und Kirche*, 1975, p. 253: "Faith is the hope of love."

96. Wilhelm Weischedel, "Vom Sinn des Gebets," in *Wirklichkeit und Wirklichkeiten* (1960), pp. 152–157 (W. Bernet, Stuttgart, 1973).

97. Quoted in M. Peitz, *Wenn wir weiterleben wollen* (1972), pp. 208f.

98. Cf. Erhard Eppler, *Ende oder Wende. Von der Machbarkeit des Notwendigen* (Stuttgart, 1975).

99. G. W. Heinemann, *Allen Bürgern verpflichtet*, Vol. 1 of *Reden und Schriften* (Frankfurt am Main, 1975), pp. 339f.